INSIDE-OUT

*Personal and Collective Life
in Israel and the Kibbutz*

Julia Chaitin

University Press of America,® Inc.
Lanham · Boulder · New York · Toronto · Plymouth, UK

Copyright © 2007 by
University Press of America,® Inc.
4501 Forbes Boulevard
Suite 200
Lanham, Maryland 20706
UPA Acquisitions Department (301) 459-3366

Estover Road
Plymouth PL6 7PY
United Kingdom

Library of Congress Control Number: 2007922677
ISBN-13: 978-0-7618-3767-1 (paperback : alk. paper)
ISBN-10: 0-7618-3767-1 (paperback : alk. paper)

Dedication

This book is dedicated with love to my husband, David, and my children Natan, Noa and Daniel, who are everything to me.

Contents

Preface

This is the book that I never knew I was going to write.

When I came home, to Israel, for a semester–long sabbatical from Nova Southeastern University in December 2004, I was not aware that 9 months later I would have a finished manuscript. What began as notes to myself, or a kind of diary written in Word, turned into a few chapters, then a collection of chapters, and finally a finished product. One chapter led to the next, and as I wrote, the chapters grew in length, intertwining with one another, drawing on one another. While in the middle of one chapter, I realized what the next, and then the next one after that would be about. One thought led to another, and yet another, and different experiences of my life, and happenings in Israel, began to come together and form a whole. I felt as if the writing was leading me, instead of the opposite. I could not have stopped the writing, if I had wanted to.

I did not know that I was going to write a book when I applied for the term off campus or even until I was half way into the writing. But during my stay at home, it became the main focus of my work as I integrated memories from the past with experiences that I was having and events occurring in Israel and in the Occupied Territories. In many ways, the writing was cathartic; it provided a positive framework for me to reflect on my growing difficulty in understanding my identity (identities) and sense of belonging to the kibbutz and to Israel. But as I wrote, it became more than an outlet for my emotions and personal questionings; it became a vehicle for understanding social and cultural phenomena and for seeing connections between behaviors and events happening in the kibbutz and those happening in wider Israeli society. I begin to understand that what I was writing could be called an autoethnography (Ellis, 2004), and that this genre meshed well not only with my personality, but with my background in qualitative research and creative writing.

I wrote this book as events were unfolding. As I readied the manuscript for press, I went through it and changed the present tense to past tense and attempted to put the events of which I write into their recent historical context. However, I did not change my original thoughts and understandings concerning the events that were unfolding in the kibbutz and Israel. This is because that would turn the book into a never–ending product, and my life still goes on.

Julia Chaitin

Negev, Israel

October 2006

Acknowledgements

This book would not have been possible without the support and help of good friends and colleagues. My heartfelt thanks go out to Dr. Shoshana Steinberg who read the chapters as soon as they were written and provided warm encouragement to write on, as well as important insights that guided me as I rethought the chapters and made needed revisions. Dr. Joyce Dalsheim read much of the book and her comments were, as always, very much on target. She helped me see what needed more elaboration and where I should further explore ideas that I only hinted at. Linda Iacovini, who was also kind enough to read the draft of the book, had important suggestions, as someone who has lived in Israel as well as the United States. She helped me understand what might need more explanation for the 'outsider' and the warmth which she offered the comments gave me the impetus to look for a publisher for the manuscript. Patrick Hiller, my graduate and research assistant, helped me with the technical preparation of the manuscript and his computer program expertise was a lifesaver. I am deeply grateful for his volunteering to help me with this aspect of the book. I would also like to acknowledge the ongoing support of Dr. J.P. Linstroth, who after reading the first number of chapters, encouraged me to continue and remained very supportive throughout the writing and publication stages. Finally, I would like to thank the Graduate School of Humanities and Social Sciences, and especially the Department of Conflict Analysis and Resolution at Nova Southeastern University in Florida, for giving me the opportunity to have a semester off campus back home in Israel that led to the writing of this book. I hope that my friends and colleagues who accompanied me on this journey will not be disappointed with the final product.

Introduction: My background and roots, some present-day thoughts, and the paths to this book

I found myself sitting engulfed in an endless cloud of cigarette smoke, wedged between five Palestinian women. Thoughts were going through my head: I have never been among people who smoke so much! Doesn't the smell bother them? How long am I going to be able to take this? I was seated between two of young women, who had to talk over me in order to converse with one another. Every now and then I noticed that the women gave each other sideways glances, and although I did not understand Arabic, I assumed that they were making occasional comments: Who is this middle-aged white woman who's sitting here? I imagined that they were asking one another: What is she doing here? Why doesn't she get up and move? Perhaps because I can be obstinate, perhaps because I wanted to connect with these Palestinian women, and/or perhaps because I saw retreat as failure on my part, I decided to continue to sit there throughout our meal, deciding that I wouldn't get up and move even if none of those women stopped speaking Arabic for a moment and turned to me to find out who I was and what I was doing in their inner circle.

It was early spring 2000 and we were having dinner at a small restaurant in Jerusalem. It was the evening before I was to co–facilitate a seminar with two Palestinian colleagues. The seminar, which was organized by the Van Leer Institute, had invited women from South Africa, Northern Ireland, Croatia and Palestine and Israel to share their experiences of living through wars, and coping with the traumas they had faced as they also worked on reconciliation with their "enemies." All of the participants were invited to this "get acquainted" dinner, before the seminar began. While I could have sat down in a "safer" spot—one by the Israeli women or by the directors of the institute and organizers of the seminar–I chose to sit down near the Palestinian participants, thinking that it would be good to make contact with them as soon as possible. Thinking that I would demonstrate to them that I, a Jewish Israeli woman, was interested in getting to know them.

A number of thoughts ran through my head: WHAT are you doing here? They obviously don't want to include you in their conversation, and it's clear that they think it's quite strange that you continue to sit there, perhaps even somewhat impolite, as they have to talk above and around you to continue their discussion. Get up, move! No, I'll stay. I'll pretend that I am an anthropologist researching a people that I do not know well.

To my credit (or perhaps due to my rebellious streak that seems to have remained with me since my teenage years), I did not get up and move. I insisted on exposing myself to massive amounts of second–hand smoke and incomprehensible conversation. I insisted on feeling what it was like to be an outsider in a place where I should have felt at home–a nice, quiet restaurant in west Jerusalem–the capital of MY country.

It was only when Choloud[1]–one of the Palestinian women–finally turned to me in English and asked my name and who I was that I felt that some progress had been made, and that my obstinacy, or tenacity, had paid off. Choloud asked me who I was, what I did, and when we discovered that we shared a common background in sociology, we had quite a nice conversation. One or two of the other women also joined in a bit, but seemed to quickly lose interest in me. It was only Choloud who kept me from being a social disaster that evening, and who did her best to engage me in some conversation.

When I returned to the hotel, I took off all of my clothes and put them in a dirty laundry pile. I remember thinking that I should have brought more clothes; that if I was going to be surrounded by chain smokers for the duration of the seminar, I was going to need a number of changes.

I remember that evening as the moment in time when I felt what it was like to be both invisible and unwanted. I remember that evening as the time when I began to realize that being a nice person, or being a peace activist, did not count for much when trying to connect to Palestinians. I remember thinking that what I had experienced that evening Palestinians experienced on a daily basis–they were invisible and unwanted; their intentions were of no or little interest to most Israelis. I remember that evening as the beginning of the end of my so unshakable Jewish–Israeli identity.

In this book I share some of my understandings of social, cultural, political, religious and economic life in Israel and the kibbutz, based on my 30+ years of life in both. My examination of social aspects of life in Israel, in general, and in the kibbutz, in particular, are not undertaken from the stand of an 'objective' researcher (if such a researcher exists), but are rather colored by my perspective, which might best be described as one that is both an insider and outsider–as someone who is inside out. This is because while I have lived in Israel and the kibbutz most of my life, I have also lived in the US for the last few years. I have come to see clearly how this physical distance from my homes has impacted the way I perceive this home, and the way in which others perceive me.

As I explore life in Israel, and on the kibbutz in this book, I also look inward, at myself. Through this writing, I am attempting to come to a deeper and clearer understanding of who I am and where I belong. Other than steadfastly holding on to my Jewish identity, I am now questioning (on a daily basis) if I am Israeli, American, a kibbutznikit (a kibbutz member), or a Zionist. Well, I'm fairly sure that I am not that anymore, not, at least, in the way that I used to define the word, and the way that it is usually defined by others–but more on that later. From this list of divergent identities, which one(s) do I want to be, and how do I want others to see me? Is it possible for me to feel that I am one of these, if others do not quite see me in that way? But perhaps most importantly–is it possible to be more than one of these, especially when the identities conflict with one another?

These questionings and self–reflections are emotionally hard work. They fill up my hours, and, to be honest, often cause my heart to race; at times, they seem to be miniature panic attacks, causing me moments of great stress and anxiety. I have engaged in the writing of this book as a way to calm my heart and to lower my anxiety, and as a way to help me work through these issues that go to the heart of my problem–Where do I belong? Where is my home? Can one have too (two) many homes? Or, even worse–Do I have a home?

Before I can explore, in depth, these questions of home and belonging, and so many other questions that are connected to this, I'd like to begin with my background, since I think that by understanding my roots, and what brought me to the kibbutz and Israel in the first place, it will be easier for you to understand why I have chosen the topics that I have for exploration in this book.

I was born in New York, but grew up in Detroit. I am the third child in a family of four (with an older brother and two sisters). I was born and raised in a Jewish family that defined itself as "secular." My zeyde, the Yiddish word for "grandfather", Yudel Mark, was a Yiddish scholar. Unfortunately, while I think that he would be proud of my academic achievements, at times I have thoughts that he is turning over in his grave since after attending Yiddish school for 14 years, I know no Yiddish–or at least no more than a handful of words that most Ashkenazi Jews know. My father spent his entire professional life involved in Jewish activities; he was a Yiddish/Hebrew school teacher, a Jewish camp director, a Jewish Federation worker, and a fundraiser for the United Jewish Appeal. My mother, on the other hand, who passed away over 16 years ago on *Pesach*[2] eve, never seemed to stress our Judaism–and while it's what we were, I never had the feeling that it comprised an important part of her identity. Unless, of course, we count the values by which she lived her life–everyone on this planet is deserving of respect and justice, regardless of their religion, the color of their skin, or ethnic background. These were core values of my Judaism–embodied in her behavior toward the people that she befriended and worked with, and the way in which she treated my friends.

As long as I can remember myself, I always knew that I was Jewish, and that this was a "good thing." I never remember feeling less than my Christian friends–of which I had many, given that we lived in a predominantly Catholic neighborhood, surrounded by churches and parochial schools. I have no memories of wanting Christmas trees or lights or presents; being Jewish was good and was who we were. It was who I was.

Until the age of 17, in addition to attending public school, I received a Jewish education at the Sholem Aleichem and Workmen's Circle schools, which began when I was three years old. In fact, the first fragment of a childhood memory that I have is sitting around a piano, when I was in the Sholem Aleichem nursery school, singing either a Shabbat or holiday song. At these schools, we were taught Yiddish, Hebrew, Jewish history and culture, holidays, and songs–none of which was religious in nature. This is because these schools saw Judaism as a cultural heritage, that embodied two languages (Yiddish, and to a lesser extent, Hebrew) and the values of democracy and social justice (see http://www.circle.org/wccjl.htm#5 for information on the Workman's Circle), while not accepting, or even relating to, the Orthodox religious aspects of Judaism.

Zionism–the ideology that the Jews needed a homeland and that this state was to be a "light unto nations"–was also an important part of that education and of the values that I was taught. I can still remember when we began learning Hebrew for the first time when I was in the fourth grade and when I learned my first Israeli folk dances. I also remember the pictures of young good–looking *Sabras* (a *sabra* is a prickly fruit, but is the term used to connote individuals who are born in Israel. There is a popular Israeli saying that the *Sabras* are rough on the outside, but sweet on the inside.). There were also photographs of *chalutzim* (pioneers) in our books about modern day Israel. They wore those funny hats, shorts and sandals, and were usually photographed either standing in an orange grove or sitting on a tractor. In those books there were no pictures of Palestinians or Arabs. For the authors of those books, and for readers like me, they were invisible. They were, simply put, not there.

In the tenth grade, I joined Habonim (Hebrew for "the builders")–a Labor Zionist youth movement that stressed *aliya* (literally means "ascent" or "going up", but is used to refer to the process of immigrating from the Diaspora to Israel) and *aliya* to kibbutz–a communal way of life. I attended meetings of our *ken* ("nest"–used to mean branch) on Friday evenings and Sunday afternoons in which we would have an *oneg Shabbat* (*Shabbat* celebration), learn Hebrew songs, dance Israeli folk dances and learn about Israel, socialism and kibbutz life. We were also involved in political activities that were non–Jewish/Israeli in nature.

I was very much a child of the 60s. I was involved in issues of social justice, such as the boycott of lettuce and grapes from California growers, who exploited migrant workers, support of the Civil Rights' movement, and protests against the Vietnam War. I also supported Jewish causes, such as working for the freeing of Soviet Jews. I was a peace activist–a peacenik. And this part of my identity has remained with me to this day, one that I do not question, one that remains a central part of my being.

My perception of the Israeli–Arab conflict–I don't remember anyone in the Jewish community speaking of Palestinians then and I certainly didn't–was simple and clear. I was a staunch supporter of peace loving Israel who was defending itself against its Arab neighbors/enemies, who I understood as having only one goal–the total destruction of Israel. I was completely unaware of the 1948 Palestinian refugee problem, having been taught that Israel had been a bare desert, empty of people, when the *chalutzim* began settling it. When I thought about the few Arabs who had lived in pre-state Israel, I always thought of them as being nomadic, so they had no real ties to the land, and I pictured them as being anti–Jewish, untrustworthy, and often murderous. That is, after all, how they were portrayed in the film, Exodus (directed and produced by Otto Preminger in 1960) one of my sources of information about Israel. So they too could be easily dismissed. The Palestinians remained invisible to me and imperceptible in that I was incapable of distinguishing them from one another, or from other Arabs.

I suppose that my ignorance and my inability to perceive the Palestinian and Arab others, my complete belief in the kibbutz–way of life, and my tendency to see things in black and white terms can be, in part, excused by my young age. After all, this kind of perception is typical of adolescence and young adulthood. And, I was espousing only what I had been taught by my elders–my *madrichim* (counselors) in Habonim and my teachers at Hebrew school.

When I graduated high school, I went on Habonim's yearlong kibbutz program, called workshop. The program was split into two groups; one went to a kibbutz in the Negev (desert) and one went to a kibbutz in the Arava (another kind of desert, in the southernmost part of the country). I was in the group that went to the very south. We spent most of our time on the kibbutz, working in different work branches, learning *Ivrit* (Hebrew) in an *ulpan* (the term used for an intensive study course in Hebrew), taking trips and nature hikes throughout the country, and participating in educational seminars on a variety of topics. While that year was not always easy for me, I loved it. It was during that year that David, who was to become my husband, and I became involved with one another and the year that I made my decision to immigrate to Israel and to settle on a kibbutz.

I made *aliya* in 1972 for a number of very noble reasons–or so they seemed at the time. I immigrated because I believed that due to centuries of persecution of the Jews, which had culminated in the tragedy of the Holocaust, the Jews needed a Jewish state and that I, as a Jew, should make my home there. Due to my firm belief in the values of democracy, egalitarianism, and socialism, I made the choice to settle on a kibbutz, although I had not picked out a specific kibbutz at that time–a minor problem for a 19 year old idealist. I arrived in Israel in May, 1972 with one hundred dollars in my pocket and two suitcases. I thought myself to be quite wealthy, again, only thoughts that a 19 year old idealist could have in 1972. I was sure that things would work out. Given that I still live in Israel, although I also lived and taught in Florida for a few years, perhaps they have. As noted above, living in Israel and kibbutz and US has made life very complicated, but it also led to the writing of this book.

After spending a year at the Hebrew University, I married David. David was born and raised in Philadelphia, had been in Habonim since he was 8 years old, and had even been the head of the movement before his *aliya*. I moved to his kibbutz in 1973, where he was a *chaver* (member) and this is where I have lived in Israel ever since.

For many years, I loved the kibbutz. Even though life was not always easy, I never doubted that the choice I had made was the right one. I hated not having an indoor toilet and shower during my first 6 months on the kibbutz, and while I was jealous of those who did have such 'luxuries', it never occurred to me that this would be a reason to give up on a communal way of life. I had a terrible time finding a job that gave me fulfillment, but I was always sure that the 'right job' was just around the corner. I was also convinced that it was my duty to work where *va'adat avodah* and the *sidran avodah* (work committee and work manager) assigned me to work; I knew that the good of the community was more important than my personal likes or dislikes. I missed American music and culture, but I immersed myself in Israeli and kibbutz culture. I loved the sense of community and caring, I loved the fact that there were many young adults to spend our afternoons and evenings with; I loved the sense of belonging and knowing that I was never alone. When I gave birth to Natan, our first, I loved the fact that there was a *beit tinokot* (baby house) and a *mitapelet tinokot* (a baby expert–caretaker) who made it clear that I call on her day or night for help; and she always did come when I called her. I miss those days, I miss that love of the kibbutz, I miss that sense of community and caring and belonging.

My son Natan and daughter Noa were born in the mid 1970s, after the Yom Kippur War, and after the Occupation had become a 'normal' part of life for both Palestinians and Israelis. Our youngest son, Daniel, was born in 1985. All of my children have been in the army. Because Natan is severely myopic, he had to volunteer for the Israel Defense Forces (IDF). As a volunteer, he served two years instead of three, which is the norm for men. Noa was in the educational branch of the army and was an officer, so her military service was longer than most women's. My youngest son, Daniel, is currently in the *tza-va* (army). He began as a *lo-chem* ("a fighter"–this refers to a soldier in a battle unit), but after he had Lasik surgery on his eyes, his medical profile was lowered and he was transferred to ordinance. I wish him with my heart and soul a boring military service. I did not have any, or rather, very few, ideological problems with Natan or Noa serving in the army; with Daniel, it's a different story. This is because, over the years, my perspectives on Zionism, Israel, the army and the Occupation have undergone a number of dramatic changes. I'll get back to this point later and often throughout the book.

All of my children received *chinuch kibbutzi* ("kibbutz education") and believe that the values that they learned during their upbringing guide their lives today. This is true of Natan who moved to the US in 1997, and who pursued a degree in finance; of Noa who lives in a commune in Tel Aviv and is a "professional volunteer" with *Hanoar haoved v'halomed* ("The working and studying youth")–a youth movement that is built on the values of human worth and dignity, social justice, Zionism, and socialism; and of Daniel who still does not know where life will take him, since he is currently busy with the military chapter of his life.

When I made *aliya*, got married and had children, I never thought that any of my children would choose to live outside of Israel. I never thought that I would be living outside of Israel. Now that Natan has decided to make his home in the United States, I tend to be much more thankful for that choice than upset by it. David remains somewhat disappointed that Natan has chosen to live outside of the country. He still believes that the home for the Jews is Israel. Given the highly dangerous political and security situation that has plagued the region for the last four years, I am thankful that at least one of my children is safe. I do not need to worry about him being caught on a bus by a suicide bomber, or becoming a target since he is in uniform. I never had these thoughts when my children were growing up. In fact, I never had them at all until recently. A not–so–small part of me feels very guilty for having brought up my children in a country that, in my opinion, has become violent and cruel, and unable to move past a mentality of war to one of peace–or at the very least–coexistence.

I came to Israel in 1972, on my own, when I was 19, with $100 in my pocket and two suitcases. I married at the age of 20 and became a kibbutz member. I worked for over 10 years in jobs which, for the most part, did not interest me, to say the least. I was a *mitapelet* ("child caretaker" or "nanny") for many different ages: toddlers, nursery school age, elementary school age; a secretary; a production worker in our small factory and the kibbutz liaison for foreign volunteers who came to see what kibbutz life was all about. After a decade of hating my jobs, I had the courage to let the *mosdot* ("institutions" or establishment) know that I could not continue working in jobs that brought me no satisfaction whatsoever, and that I needed to find a profession that would resonate with who I was, if I were to remain sane. At that time, I was full of hope that I would be able to find a profession that would contribute to the kibbutz.

In order to find this 'perfect world', I went back to school in 1985. I earned my B.A. in Behavioral Sciences in 1989, my M.A. in Organizational Psychology in 1995. I was conferred my PhD in 2000 in Social Psychology. All degrees came from Ben Gurion University of the Negev–which, in many ways, became my second home. Since the end of my Bachelors degree, I have been involved in social science research, which began with the study of the long term psychosocial effects of the Holocaust on survivors and their descendants, and on German Christians, born after World War II. Since my Masters' days, I have known that the academic life was the life for me.

While this journey has been wonderful for me–from both a personal and professional standpoint–it has taken me away even further from my kibbutz. As life would have it, my kibbutz does not need a social psychologist researcher or a full–time peace activist. But this is what I know and want to do. Since the mid 1990s, I have been an *ovedet chutz* ("outside worker"–used to denote a kibbutz member who works off the kibbutz, and deposits his/her salary into the kibbutz bank account). The more I work outside, the less I am connected to the kibbutz. The less I am connected, the more I prefer being on the outside; hence, giving rise to some of my inside out complications. These complications have not only touched upon my relationship with the kibbutz, and with most of its *chaverim*, but with my family and close friends as well.

I came to Israel to make the desert bloom, to lead a socialist life, to be part of that light unto nations and to fulfill the Jewish dream of helping to continue to build the Jewish state. I left my mother and father, my two sisters and brother, my friends and the life that I had known in the United States. I did so willingly, and with a sense of purpose. I never doubted that my decision to make *aliya* was the right one. I knew that I was going to make Israel my home forever.

That was in 1972–a lifetime ago. Over the years, having lived the socialist and Jewish 'dream', I have come to have more complex and often contradictory feelings about the choices I have made, my home, my identity and my life. I have come to accept these complex and contradictory feelings as being part of who I am, though I do not think that I have come to embrace them (yet). Some examples of this complexity: Even though I have always been a deeply secular person, I became very emotional and cried when Daniel had his bar–mitzvah. Even though I abhor war and the militaristic way of life, so characteristic of Israel, I never miss our kibbutz ceremony for *Yom Hazikron* (Memorial Day) and I stand there with tears in my eyes as the *chaverim* and *banim* (sons) of the fallen light torches in their memory. Even though I believe that we must find a way to share this land with our Palestinian neighbors, I sing Hatikva ("The Hope"–Israel's national anthem) in a clear and loud voice, often also shedding a tear while I sing. Even though I consider the kibbutz and Israel my home, I hate what they have become, and manage to fit easily into America.

It's complicated–and this is what this book is about.

Notes

1. All the names of people used in this book are pseudonyms, unless they are famous people.
2. Pesach is the Hebrew word for Passover.

Chapter 1 or The dreaded identity crisis that has been brewing becomes full–blown

I came back to Israel and the kibbutz in late December 2004, from my university in the US, to spend a semester home and to teach my courses on line, after having been gone for three and a half months. It was both wonderful and difficult. It is home, yet so much less a part of me then it was a few years ago. Everything is familiar, yet somehow foreign; my wish to belong argues with my wish to be a visitor. When I am in Ft. Lauderdale, I yearn to be 'home'; when I am here, I long for the US, though not necessarily in southern Florida–a place that often strikes me as wasteland, the Mecca of the superficial and heartless.

Our flight from London arrived at Ben–Gurion Airport or *Nut–bug*, as it is called for short in Hebrew. We arrived in terminal three–the new terminal that was opened up in mid September of 2004, after I had already returned to Florida for my second year of teaching. Terminal one–the old terminal–was Israel. Terminal three is *chutz le'aretz* ("abroad")–fancy, shmancy–not Israeli, yet very Israeli in its design. I came back to a place that I had never left. Familiar, yet foreign; Israel with a door to and from the world.

After the endless walk to passport control, getting a crick in my neck as I tried to take in the new terminal with its marble walls, murals, and art/tourist posters, to the baggage area, and through customs, I came out into a sea of people. Israelis. This was familiar–people pushing to get through to the loved ones they were meeting, not listening to the security guard who kept telling them to stay behind the line. David came up from the left; I didn't see him at first. A smile, a kiss and a hug and another endless walk to the new parking garage and to the dirty kibbutz car. Kibbutz cars are always dirty; it's just a matter of degree. This one probably wouldn't be considered dirty by David or kibbutz standards–you could make out that it was white and the floor mats and trunk weren't full of dirt from the fields.

The drive home in the dark, after three flights, three airports, and 24 hours of being in a semi–conscious state had a dreamlike quality. I knew where I was, but still had to keep asking David where we were–how much further to the kibbutz? The darkness and the tiredness made it too difficult for me to get my bearings. We stopped at a gas station with a rest stop that is half an hour from the kibbutz. On our way out of the parking lot, a soldier was hitchhiking. I rolled down the window and asked: "Where are you going?" "To Masmiah" I looked at David, because I had no idea where that was, or if we were going by there, though I know exactly where it is and that we had already passed it forty five minutes ago. I knew, but didn't know. David said: "Sorry–we're going the other way" and the soldier smiled and said "thank you" and we drove off.

When we entered the kibbutz and stopped at the side of the road by the sidewalk that leads to our house to unload my suitcases, I remembered the kibbutz. There was an overpowering smell of cow manure; it always hits you when you've been away for a while. Five dogs ran up to the car to sniff around. I could see into my neighbors' houses and see my women neighbors, through their kitchen windows, washing dishes and cleaning up from dinner. I pulled my two suitcases, backpack and laptop to our house. Daniel was waiting for me, standing in the living room. I put down everything and we gave each other a very, big warm hug. I then moved the suitcases a bit and said that I needed another one. Big, warm hug number two. Daniel misses me, I thought, and that made my heart skip a beat. He looked wonderful.

I was in my home, but couldn't say that "I was home." Out of habit, I picked up the dish rag and began wiping down the granite countertop. For some reason, that's always the first thing that I do when I return home. I separate the dish drainer from its tray, and spill the dirty water that I know will be collected there into the sink; David rarely notices it and Daniel never notices it. This is my welcome home ritual to myself.

Jet lag the first night, slept the second and jet lag the third and fourth. I turned night into day, though I didn't sleep in the day either. I was happy that I now had an 'official' reason for not sleeping, but I know that this is basically an excuse; even when I do not travel for 26 consecutive hours from the airport to home, I am not a good sleeper. I spend too much of my days and nights thinking. I have come to the conclusion that it is better to think less and sleep more.

I went to Ben Gurion University twice during my first week home–once to hear Amia Lieblich give a talk about her latest book (2004) which is on women in 'non-conventional' marriages. It was hard for me to concentrate on the lecture and so I was a bit disappointed. I was disappointed since I have always loved Professor Lieblich's work and have always found it to be engaging. Perhaps it was me? The second time I went to the university to participate in a seminar on art–based qualitative research. I went to absorb some of the BGU culture that I love so much, and to meet up with friends–Lea, Dan, Shoshana, Eitan, June, Orit–and to pretend that, once again, I belonged there.

But I didn't belong there–I once did, but now I have become a visitor, a welcome visitor, but a visitor nonetheless. I went to school at BGU for 13 years and taught there for 5 years, but it is no longer mine. The Israeli Center for Qualitative Methodologies (ICQM), which I established with Lea in her tiny office, was once my home. I was its co–founder and co–director, but it is no longer mine, though my name is still on the sign outside the door to the office. For some reason, they haven't gotten around to changing it.

The identity crisis of where I belong followed me to Beer Sheva. I didn't get the job offer that I had worked so hard for from BGU and so I came to NSU to have an academic career. This move was so much more than a geographical one, as it moved me away physically, academically, mentally and emotionally from what was my home for so many years: Israel, the kibbutz and BGU.

I had so much that I wish I could share with my friends here, but when I began to tell them, I got cold feet; I sensed somehow that I wouldn't be able to express myself, or that they wouldn't understand what I was going through or that they would judge me negatively. I stopped myself and phrased things in a way that avoided the sharing. Once a close friend of mine told me that I have the tendency to do this; to talk 'as if' sharing, while not really sharing. I didn't feel that I could share with these good friends the real things that I was feeling. I was afraid to tell them that I was no longer certain that Israel is my home, even though I cannot picture not living here. I was afraid to say out loud that I am not sure that I want to remain here, on the kibbutz. I was afraid that once I say these things out loud, I would lose this home and these friends forever. I wouldn't be able to keep what I have, though I don't really feel that I have it anymore. Saying it out loud seems to give it magical powers, and could jeopardize everything that I feel is somewhat over, yet am afraid to let go of.

I knew that I was presenting a false self to these people that I hold dear. I was not being honest with them. I hold David dear, but even though we discussed these issues, it was very difficult for me to do so, since from our conversations I understood how differently he sees and *feels* his connection to the kibbutz, and to the country. The identity crisis was upon me, but I still wanted to hold it in abeyance.

When I got home, I took a brisk walk in the morning, worked in the garden for an hour or so, smiled at *chaverim* (members) on the sidewalks as I went to the store, or to pick up my mail and newspaper, and would say "*Shalom, ma nishma* (Hi–how are you?), yes it's good to be back, yes, it's great, yes David's happy and it's good to be here for Daniel. Yes, it's great." I worked in the garden and thought "this is great" but I felt it so much less so than I remembered it in my imagination, there, in Fort Lauderdale.

During the art–based qualitative research seminar, I took out my journal, that I bought on sale at Borders, and began writing notes from the lecture in Hebrew. Lea, my dear friend, who is chair of the ICQM that was running the seminar, leaned over and said to me: "You're writing in Hebrew from left to right." I smiled and said to her: "It's a sign of my identity crisis." Lea laughed and said: "I understand" and I responded with an upward wave of my hand and a laugh "Right now it's in the heavens."

Lea had taken a sabbatical by herself when she went to work with colleagues in New Zealand and Australia for a number of months on different qualitative research projects. She knew what it was like to live apart from a husband and family for awhile, because of a job. As we were drinking coffee over the break, catching up with one another, and talking about this and that, all of a sudden, Lea said to me, unsolicited as it were, "You know, it's important that you come home before it gets too easy to live apart. If you live apart for too long, things could get complicated. You need to come home now. Things will work out if you are here." I smiled and said: "It's not that easy" and let it go at that. For the meantime.

Chapter 2 or New Years with the family and visiting Daniel in the army

On New Year's Eve, the first weekend that I was back, Noa and her boyfriend, Asaf, came down from Tel Aviv to the kibbutz for dinner. They both looked wonderful and it was a lovely evening. We sat around the dining room table for a long time, talking about this and that, laughing, feeling good to be with one another. The last thing that Noa said before they left was: *"Tov kshe yesh eema babayit"* (dual translation: It's good to have a mother at home–It's good when mom is home).

The next day, I realized that we had not talked "politics;" we hadn't once mentioned the *kibbush* (Occupation), the separation fence/wall, or the *sarbanim* (refuseniks–soldiers who refuse to serve in the Occupied Territories). I can't remember the last time that a conversation of this sort did not take place. Now I wonder whether we all unconsciously decided not to discuss it, since it's a topic that we always end up disagreeing about. Perhaps it was our desire to make sure that this first family dinner since my homecoming would be very peaceful, one where we could just enjoy each other's company without getting into heated arguments about whether or not the separation fence is a good thing or a bad thing, or whether if soldiers refuse to obey an order–such as serving in the Occupied Territories, will this herald the end of Israeli democracy? Perhaps I didn't bring up the issues since I feel that my position falls on deaf ears and brings discomfort into our conversations.

The night after the visit, on the news, there was a report about an orthodox Israeli soldier who called to his fellow soldiers to refuse to participate in the dismantling of an illegal Jewish settlement in the West Bank as the dismantling was being carried out. Some of the settlers tried to take a soldier's gun away from him, and so he shot into the air to scare them off. Was this an example of Israeli democracy at work?

On the first day of the New Year, David and I went to visit Daniel in his *motzav* (outpost)–15 minutes from Tel Aviv, and just over the green line, in the *shtachim* (territories–in this case, specifically the West Bank). The evening before, David asked me if I was willing to go. "Of course I want to go–why do you ask?" "Because it's in the *shtachim*, and you don't think that Israelis should be in the *shtachim*." This is one of David's 'subtle' ways of telling me that he doesn't agree with my politics. I pretended that I didn't understand the barb, and, for a second time, avoided talking politics at home since I had been back;

it's a futile exercise and just frustrates us both. "Why wouldn't I go visit Daniel? Of course I want to go." And I left it at that.

When we got close to the *motzav*, we had to pass a checkpoint, and drive approximately 10 kilometers roundabout to be able to take the back road into the base. Though there were no signs of any Palestinians, I was nervous and had a stomachache. We couldn't enter the *motzav* via the main road since this road goes through a religious settlement and it would have been disrespectful to drive through their community on the *Shabbat* (on *Shabbat* driving a car is against Jewish religious law). Daniel gave us directions to his base: from the highway, a kilometer or so before the checkpoint, there is a break in the metal security bar; you will see a dirt road and containers down below. That is the *motzav*. The buildings in the *motzav* are shipping containers. So, my baby, Daniel, was now living in a box.

Daniel met us at the entrance to the base. He was dressed in a black t–shirt, sweatpants, and had thongs on his feet. Since it was *Shabbat*, and he wasn't on duty, he didn't need to be in uniform and he was allowed to wear whatever he wanted. But he had his M–16 slung across his left shoulder, crossing his stomach and hip. I remembered that when we went to visit him in late August, at another base in the northern part of the country, and had taken him out for lunch, he had to eat with his rifle nestled between his legs. Then, when I asked him if he couldn't put it aside while he ate, he gave me a strange look and said no.

Daniel's tiny box had four bunk beds, four metal side cabinets, an un-plugged television that didn't receive any stations, and a radio–tape. There was a poster of a popular Israeli comedian and a calendar on the opposite wall. Since on *Shabbat* soldiers only do jobs that are absolutely necessary, that is kitchen and guard duty, most of them had the day off. The guys who had remained on the base were playing soccer. Other than their voices, which periodically drifted into our box, and music which was playing from the radio, it was quiet.

Daniel opened up the package of goodies that we had brought with us from the kibbutz. All soldiers who are *bnei kibbutz* (children of the kibbutz) receive a "care package" once a month. Daniel sat on the bottom of his bunk bed and we sat facing him, on the bottom of the bunk bed across from him, our knees almost touching. As Daniel ate two small candy bars, he told us about the base and the settlement across the way. We talked about how he was in the process of asking his commanding officer to let him move from this tiny base to headquarters, where he would have the opportunity to have a more interesting job (that is, anything other than kitchen duty). As we discussed Daniel's plans, this brought up memories for David about his own *tiranut* (basic training) and army service, and how much he had hated it back then.

David had never been much of a soldier, though he served in the regular army for 9 months and then did another 22 years of *miluim* (reserve duty). At times, his reserve duty took him away from home for over a month–which made it difficult for all of us. The worst times were when Natan and Noa were little and David had *miluim* during the holidays, and when he was called up during the first Gulf War, and Daniel, Noa, Natan and I had to go scurrying into our sealed room without him, putting on our gas masks and waiting for the all clear siren.

David recounted a story of his *tiranut* during our visit with Daniel. He remembered how once his unit was sent to another base where they had to construct a temporary stage for a large ceremony that was to take place there. The stage was made of Bailey bridge pieces that the soldiers had to carry and make into the stage. David recalls how bitterly cold it was, and how there were no provisions made for them to sleep or eat. "We were basically slaves for those days." Daniel smiled, thinking about how different his *tiranut* had been. Now there are rules that the officers must follow–such as making sure that their soldiers have at least 6 hours of sleep a night and that they always have food provisions. Today, soldiers have cell phones and there is rarely a day that a soldier cannot talk with their families and friends.

When Daniel's officer called him outside for a moment, Daniel stood up, put on his gun, and went out to talk to him. A.A. Milne's poem (1927) ran through my head, only this time, with slightly different words: Wherever he goes, there's always his gun, there's always his gun and he.

We stayed for about an hour and a half, gave kisses and said goodbye. We drove out of the *shtachim* and back into Israel. The darkening sky and the motion of the car rocked me to sleep, and I slept almost until we made it home. When I woke up I said to David: "I'm sorry for not being able to stay awake and keep you company." "That's fine; I'm just glad that you're here. Daniel wouldn't have invited me to come visit him on his base, if you hadn't been here."

Chapter 3 or Occupation, refugees and academic life, with a side of falafel and chips

My friend, Joyce, an anthropologist, called me on the phone on Tuesday morning to talk about her research on Jewish settlers in Gaza, before the planned disengagement. As a self-defined "left–wing peacenik," at times it was emotionally difficult for her to listen to the settlers' ideologies that so contrasted with hers, yet, on a personal level, she found them to be "very nice people" who opened up their homes to her on a regular basis and invited her to stay for *Shabbat*. Alongside this work, she felt a need to become much more active in peace efforts.

As part of her desire to attend activities that dealt with the Occupation[1], and since she knows about my deep interest in the topic, Joyce invited me to go with her to the Hebrew University to hear a panel discussion on a new book, *Confronting the Occupation*. This book is based on anthropological research carried out by Maya Rosenfeld (2004) in the Deheishe refugee camp during the mid 1990s. In her study, Rosenfeld looked at issues of labor, education and political activism among three generations of Palestinian refugee families. The panel was comprised of two Jewish Israeli anthropologists, Dr. Efrat Ben Ze'ev and Prof. Emanuel Marx, and a Palestinian–Israeli sociologist, Dr. Salim Tamari.

Unfortunately, Emanuel Marx stole the show. I was unhappy that his name reminded me of my father's name–Emanuel Mark–given how his talk appeared to stand in direct contrast to my father's views. Marx made remarks that I found to be offensive; he spoke from a position that I can only describe as one of arrogance, giving "scholarly and expert" recommendations about how to resolve the Palestinian refugee "problem."

I have been wondering why the plight of the Palestinian refugees is always referred to as a "problem"–I cannot escape my associations with the "Jewish problem" that faced the Nazis during the Second World War. I have found myself thinking about who has the authority to define when another people become a "problem." In his talk, Marx stated that it would be wrong for the Israeli government to allow the Palestinian refugees to return to their original (pre–Israel) homes, since this would constitute a resettlement of the people who had already been resettled at least once, and who did not need this traumatic experience again! Therefore, it would be "best" for the Palestinians to remain where they are, as not to cause them further pain. This struck me as a true example of how arrogance and disregard can be reframed into a manifest position of 'care' or 'empathy' for the other–in this case, the Palestinians. Emanuel Marx, cast as a reactionary version of James Taylor (1971), sings to the Palestinians: *You've gotta friend*. . .

It was hard to decide what was more amazing–Marx's remarks or the fact that no one from the audience or the panel really challenged him on this issue, letting it hang in the air, and as a result, lending his claim legitimacy. In all fairness to the others, I remained quiet as well. Later on, I felt shame for this silence.

The seminar uncovered two opposing faces of Israeli academia–on the one hand, there are the *yafei nefesh* ("gentle souls"). This term, which carries with it an undertone of ridicule and belittlement, is often used by right wing advocates to describe left wing, liberals. Today Israelis who speak of peace and co-existence are seen as being dangerously naïve concerning the *real* intentions of the Palestinians. Because of this naiveté, the *yafei nefesh* are often perceived and portrayed as being ultimately dangerous to the survival of Israel. The *yafei nefesh* in the room were represented on the stage by Maya Rosenfeld and Efrat Ben Ze'ev–two Jewish Israeli women scholars who speak out against the Occupation. The other face of Israeli academia, the one that troubles me, includes those academics that support and perpetuate the militaristic, governmental line. Their mantra is: We have studied the Arabs, we understand the Arabs, let us explain them to you, some of our best friends are Arabs, we know what is best for them.

The polarization of the camps in Israeli academia also reflects the polarization that has characterized Israeli society for the last decade, certainly since the assassination of Yitzchak Rabin in November 1995. (*How could this have happened over 10 years ago? I believe that the sadness of those days will remain etched in my heart forever.*) At the time of the Jerusalem seminar, Israeli news was completely pre–occupied (no pun intended) with the issue of disengagement from the Gaza Strip and the dismantling of Jewish settlements there, and perhaps later on in the West Bank, where most of the Jewish settlements outside of the *Kav Hayarok* (Green Line) are located.

The big news in Israel during the early part of 2005 focused on the calls from the leadership of the religious Zionist right to IDF soldiers to disobey orders if called upon to dismantle Jewish settlements in the territories. In mid–January 2005, 60 rabbis called on soldiers to refuse to dismantle Jewish settlements, stating that it went against Jewish law. There were a number of reserve officers and soldiers (the number ranges from 30 to 10,000, depending on the source) who signed a letter stating their intent to refuse to partake in such actions. In response, the then Chief of Staff, Moshe Ya'alon, announced that any officer who did not retract his name would be stripped of his rank and ousted from the IDF (Aronson, 2005).

The debate over *Sarbanut* (refusing to follow IDF orders) is not new to Israel. Up to now, the *sarbanim* (refuseniks) came from the left–soldiers who have refused to serve in the Occupied Territories. Many of these *sarbanim* have been jailed in military prisons and been identified as near-traitors by many Israelis (Kidron, 2004; Courage to Refuse–www.seruv.org.il). I have supported these refusenik soldiers, by sending email messages telling them that they are not alone, making modest monetary donations, and by writing letters to governmental and military authorities to release these men. I have written no such letters of support to the right-wing, religious *sarbanim*.

Over the past 10 years, since Rabin's assassination, there have been signs and expressed fears that Israel is moving to a civil war–or in Hebrew– *milchement achim*–which literally means, a "war between brothers." This is a war that will be between Jews, a war that will take place within the family, so to speak. If this prophecy becomes a reality, this will be a war between democratic rule and theocratic rule, between Jews who see Jews as people and Jews who see the Palestinians as less–than–people, between Jews who believe that *Midinat Yisrael* (the State of Israel) is for all of its citizens and Jews who believe that *Eretz Yisrael* (the Land of Israel) belongs only to the Jews. I have a growing sense of doom that if such a war breaks out, this will be a bloody and protracted war, since we have become such a militarized society and are experts at war.

But Israeli society is too complex to be only depressing or scary. A day after my visit to Jerusalem, on channel two, one of the major Israeli television stations, there was a report about a Palestinian photographer, Ahmed Jadallah, who has won international prizes for his photographs of Gaza during the last *Intifada*. In 2003, while Jadallah, who works for Reuters, was filming a street scene, Israeli tank fire opened on pedestrians. The photographer was hit by the blast, and fell to the ground unconscious for a few moments. When he awoke, he asked people who had come to his aid to give him his camera. He then shot photos of the carnage, as he lay bleeding on the ground. One of these photos (see the website from the Nooderlich photo festival of 2004 that provides background about Jadallah and features a number of his pictures: http://www. noorderlicht.com/eng/fest04/friesmuseum/jadallah) captured a man who had gone to the grocery store, got caught in the crossfire, and was killed. The man lay dead next to Jadallah. This picture won the photographer a top international news award and his photos were even showcased in an Israeli exhibit of top documentary photographs from around the world. Israel is indeed a strange place. . . .

Later, when Jadallah was taken to an Israeli hospital for treatment, he shared a room with Jewish Israelis who had been wounded in a terror attack. Because he could not move, one of the Jewish patients, who lived in a settlement in the West Bank, came to his bedside and fed him, gave him water, and kept him company. On the day that he was released from the hospital, the photographer told his new friend: "If we can lie side by side here in a hospital and be friends, we can manage on the outside." Israel is indeed an extraordinary and a strange place.

After the seminar was over, before heading home, Joyce and I stopped for falafel in a hole in the wall in *Issawiya*, an Arab neighborhood located in East

Jerusalem, near Mount Scopus, the location of the Hebrew University, that had been occupied in the Six Day War. The falafel is delicious, and comes with *chips* (French fries), humus, *techina* (sesame seed paste) and salads and costs 7 NIS each. There is a fancier place down the block, but the locals say that the falafel in the hole in the wall is better. I treated Joyce to 'dinner' and we pulled out two white plastic chairs from the 'store' and sat on the sidewalk. A large truck had pulled up in front and there was Arabic music on the radio. We ate our falafel, swaying to the music. Joyce said: "I brought you here so you could have the full Israeli experience."

I have recurring labyrinthitis–an inflammation of the inner ear that causes me to be dizzy and off balance. Perhaps my country is also suffering from recurring and long–term labyrinthitis–and given that it's viral, there is no known treatment that can help. . . .

Notes

1. The Occupation refers to Israel's occupation of the West Bank and the Gaza Strip, areas conquered by Israel in the Six Day War in June 1967.

Chapter 4 or Cows, capitalism and kibbutz economics

In Spring 2005, while the country was torn over the issue of disengagement from Gaza, including the dismantling of Jewish settlements, and the effects that it is having on our society (see chapter 3), on the kibbutz, the talk on the *midrachot* (sidewalks) was about disengaging the *refet* (the milking barn) from the kibbutz.

Some background: In the good old days, Israel was a socialist state, and all of the major industries and markets were government and cooperative driven and run. Israel has become much more capitalistic in its economic policies since the early 1980s when inflation was extremely high (Econstats: http://www. econstats.com/weo/C079V025.htm), government policies changed, leading to less government control, and when it was clear that the old Socialist bubble had burst. While the milk market was not impacted early on to the extent that other economic sectors were (Mellul, 1984), in recent years, this has changed and there have been a number of reforms in this sector as well.

The Israeli Ministry of Environment, in conjunction with the milk industry, revised its rules about physical and health standards for *refatot*. In order to meet these new standards, the *refet* at the kibbutz was informed that it needed to invest approximately five and a half million NIS (1,250,800 USD at the time) in the near future in order to keep producing and selling milk. If the kibbutz does not invest the money, then we were told to expect large fines. This would essentially put the *refet* out of business and negatively impact the overall economic situation of the kibbutz, which has been suffering from fiscal problems for many years. In the spring of 2005, the kibbutz faced two choices: to invest the money–which it did not have–or to sell the *refet*. The economic winds, as expressed by the kibbutz institutions, were blowing in the direction of selling.

The *refet* has seen its ups and downs. When I came to the kibbutz in the early 1970s, it was considered a "cool" place to work, where young men (and now and then a young woman) would milk three times a day in terrible conditions–with the most ungodly shift beginning at around three o'clock in the morning. The *tzevet* (team/staff) was perceived as being "tight" and comprised of "real" kibbutz members.

Over the years, the *refet* has turned into an unpopular *anaf* (a work branch). It has become impossible to find kibbutz members who want to make it their permanent workplace, and so more and more of the *tzevet* is comprised of young adults who are on the kibbutz for a few months before heading off for a trek to the East (usually India, Thailand, etc.) or to South America. The other workers are comprised of paid Thai and Chinese workers who come to the kibbutz for extended periods of time to make money to send back to their families at home, or Bedouin from neighboring areas.

One of the *vatikim,* ran the *refet* for many years, before his legs and eyes gave out (*vatik* translates to "senior," *vatikim* is the plural; in kibbutz jargon, *vatikim* is the term used to designate the founding kibbutz members). However, he continues to be involved in the *anaf*; barefoot and wearing his dirty blue work clothes, he drives his muddy motorized cart along the sidewalks of the kibbutz, carrying equipment and food to and from the *refet* and he pops in for daily visits to see how things are going.

For the last two years, there has been only one permanent member in the *refet*, and she is the manager. For a host of reasons, many kibbutz members do not hold this manager in high regard. There are those who think of her as a woman who often gets herself into unnecessary complicated situations, as someone who 'causes trouble' and makes much too much noise when she does not like a particular kibbutz decision. For years, the new *refet* manager made public proclamations of wanting to run the *anaf* and these were usually met with blatant scorn by the economic leadership, as well as by other members. It was only in mid 2004, after she completed a degree in management, and when it became clear that no other member was interested in the job, that the *hanhala* (management) voted her in as *merakezet harefet* (in charge of the *refet*).

The manager is not only the first woman on the kibbutz who was elected to manage the *refet*, but also the first woman to be elected to run any *anaf yatzrani* (productive work branch–e.g. factories, field crops, etc.). She heads a small staff of temporary workers, who are *bnei meshek* (young adults who born on the kibbutz) who have not committed to remaining on the kibbutz for any length of time over a year. Giving her the job appeared to me to be a sign that the status of the *refet* had officially drastically declined and that it is no longer considered a serious *anaf*. This is not only because the manager is a woman, but because of how she is perceived by the community.

But the gender issue cannot be ignored. The kibbutz has what I would characterize as a notoriously bad record in gender equality; since its establishment in the mid 1940s, there has *never* been a woman *merakez meshek* (economic director–the most important and powerful job in the kibbutz), there was *never* a woman *gizbar* (treasurer) except for 6 months back in the 1960s when a woman held the job temporarily, and there has *never* been a woman in charge of any of the money making *anafim*. For nearly 60 years, the kibbutz has remained faithful to its manifest ideology that there is equality between the sexes in running of the kibbutz and in work branches and its not–so–latent–hard–to–miss procedures of extremely rarely, if ever, offering such positions to one of the women members. "No woman ever wanted the job" is a common comment made by the male leadership and male and female followers.

There are two exceptions to this unwritten rule that I know about. Once there was some talk of offering one of the women the job of *merakezet meshek*, though no firm offer ever came of it, and once I was offered the job of *gizbar*, after I completed my doctorate. This made me realize that it was only after a woman had a doctorate that she could seriously be offered a position of handling the kibbutz's money, whereas, men were seen as being suited for this position, by virtue of their...?

But back to the cows. In a meeting in early spring, the *hanhala kalkalit* (economic directorate) had a meeting about the *refet* which lasted for the morning hours. David and one of my good friends were members of the committee, and they separately shared with me some of what had gone on. It was interesting hearing their takes on the meeting, since they see the world, in general, and the kibbutz, in particular, in very different ways. However, they both agreed that the meeting had been a very difficult and emotional one. While only two members of the committee came out and said that it made most sense to sell the *refet*, there was quiet consensus that all of the other *hanhala* members were of the same opinion. David told me that the manager of the *refet* was distraught and kept saying: "The *chaverim* (members) will never agree to this. There will be a revolt against the *hanhala kalkalit*." My friend told me that a number of the male members of the directorate were condescending and that scorn and contempt could be heard in their voices when they addressed the manager. David told me that he thought the manager was living in a fantasy world, viewing the *refet* as it was in stories from its heyday, in the 1960s and 1970s, before she had lived on the kibbutz. He found it sad. I wondered what he had said during their committee meeting.

When David came home from the meeting, he told me: "There will be a lot to write about in our weekly newsletter." What he meant was that not only would there be articles written about the *refet* and the *hanhala kalkalit* in the newsletter, but that it would be *the* topic of discussion around the kibbutz. And sure enough, the next day, throughout the kibbutz–on the doors to the dining room, the clinic, the laundry, the main office, by the mailboxes, etc. etc. Celia had put up signs on orange paper that said: *Gam harefet neged hahitnatkut. Pratim etzel hahanhala hakalkalit* ("The *refet* is also against disengagement– details from the economic directorate").

The choice of orange paper was symbolic in that orange had become the color of the opposition to the disengagement from Gaza; Jewish Israeli settlers wore orange t–shirts, flew orange flags on their cars (some still do even though the disengagement occurred in August 2005), and even donning orange stars on their clothing–reminiscent of the yellow star that Jews were forced to wear during the Holocaust in many countries under Nazi occupation. This was used to symbolize the Jewish–Israelis' victimhood and to broadcast their belief that they were being thrown out of their homes, only this time not by others, but by Jews.

And so, everything is connected–disengagement from the *refet* was associated with disengagement from Gaza. Just as the Jews were being 'thrown out' of Gaza, the cows were being thrown out of the kibbutz. And this is bad–bad because it goes against the 'Zionist' values of the country and bad because it goes against the 'socialist' and 'Zionist' values of the kibbutz. Or so the manager of the *refet* and the religious Zionist Jews who believe in *Eretz Yisrael Hashlema* (Greater Israel) would have us think.

In the newsletter, which came out on the following Friday after the meeting of the *hanhala hakalkalit*, the editor included some jokes which looked at capitalism through cows. Below follows "A few ways to manage a *refet* in a capitalistic world":

> Classic capitalism–you have two cows. You sell one and buy a bull. Your herd grows and you make more money. You retire and live off of your earnings.
> American capitalism–You have two cows. You sell one and force the other to produce four times as much milk. You are surprised when the cow dies of exhaustion.
> French capitalism–You have two cows. You go out on strike since you don't have three.
> German capitalism–You have two cows. You order them to make twice as much milk. When they don't do what you ordered, you shoot one of them. The second cow produces four times as much milk.
> Italian capitalism–You have two cows, but you don't know where they are. You go out to lunch.
> Russian capitalism–You have two cows. You count them and discover that you have four. You count again and discover that you have eight cows. You count them again and discover that you have sixteen cows. You stop counting cows and open up another bottle of vodka.
> Chinese capitalism–You have two cows and 300 people who milk them. You declare that there is full employment and production is high. You forbid the media to report the numbers.
> Israeli capitalism–You have 2 cows. One belongs to the *Histadrut* (the major Israeli labor union) and one to the State. They are both on strike. You buy milk from the US with the money that the US gave in financial aid.

(My addition) Our kibbutz socialism/ capitalism–You have 300 cows, one *chavera* (member) who runs the business, five *bnei meshek* and two *Thailandim* (Hebrew for people from Thailand–usually refers to foreign workers hired by agricultural communities) who do the work. You have one *hanhala kalkalit* which makes the financial decisions concerning the *anaf*. The *chavera* espouses socialism, Zionism, the good old days and revolt, and hangs up signs about this throughout the kibbutz, while the *hanhala kalkalit* plans to close the *refet*, all the while treating *the chavera* with contempt, even though they voted her in to run the place. While Israel planned for disengagement from Gaza, our kibbutz dealt with disengagement from the cows. As the debate grew more and more heated, and more and more public, the *chaverim* (members) were happy since there was now a new topic for discussion on the *midrachot* and there was what to read in the weekly newsletter. While no one was tending to them, the cows got out of their pens and were seen wandering around the kibbutz. . . .

Chapter 5 or Coming 'home', memories of childhood, equality and parking spaces

Natan, my oldest son, who now lives in the United States, came to visit for two weeks in January 2005 after not having been 'home' for four and a half years. On the second day of his visit, after we ate lunch in the dining room with David, and David went back to work in the *mifal* (factory), Natan asked that we take a walk around the kibbutz "to see what was new." We wandered, with no plan in mind, and as we walked, Natan made comments about what was 'new', that is, hadn't been there over four years ago, to the best of his recollection, and what was 'old', that is, he had a memory of it. He tried to remember exactly how long he had lived on the kibbutz ("almost 20 years?") and to see if things looked the way in which they were etched in his memory.

We walked over to the area that had once been the kibbutz elementary school when Natan was a child. For the last 15 years, the children have gone to a regional school–a 15 minute bus ride from the kibbutz. The school serves the kibbutzim of our regional council, which is comprised of 26 kibbutzim and *moshavim* (a type of agricultural settlement). But when Natan was growing up, all education, except for formal high school studies, took place on the kibbutz. This is because, up until the 1990s, relatively, there were many members–over 200–and many children, since most members were married and had either three or four children. In the decade of the 1970s, the years when my older children were born, there were about 20 births per year; Daniel's year in 1985 was also large with 22 (!) births.

Up until the mid to late 1980s, there was little to no *aziva* ("leaving", which refers to members giving up their membership and leaving the kibbutz, usually to live in the city). That meant that Natan and Noa grew up in the heyday of the kibbutz, when the oldest members were barely in their fifties, and the elementary school on the kibbutz was run exclusively by kibbutz–trained teachers and *mitaplot* ("caretakers"–nannies; all women). These were the years when the kibbutz was filled with children's laughter and screams, and strewn with bicycles and toys. *Hachinuch hakibbutzi* (kibbutz education) was considered to be *the* pinnacle of education in Israel; an education based on revered values such as democracy, socialism, equality, Zionism, and physical connectedness to the land, which translated into valuing an agricultural way of life. At that time, it was politically incorrect to mention out loud that the *chinuch hakibbutzi* tended to advocate a form of equality that ultimately stressed strict conformity for all the children, who had equal opportunities to rise to "the height of grass."

Here is one example of how equality was defined then for children: all of the children received their clothes from the *matpeira* (the sewing workshop in which a small group of members made the children's clothes). Each child was entitled to the same amount and type of clothes–*b'gdei boker* (morning clothes)– these were clothes to be worn during the day when the children were in the *batei yeladim* (children's house); clothes to play in and get dirty in. And then there were *b'gdei erev* (evening clothes)–for the kids to wear when they came home to be with their family. The children also received two sets of *b'gdei Shabbat* ("Shabbat clothes") that were for *Shabbat*, holidays or special occasions, such as bar–mitzvahs or weddings.

The distribution of clothes was even more detailed than this, for arriving at a system of equality is not easy. For example, each child was given X number of flannel shirts, and Y number of pajamas. Now if a child did not like flannel shirts, but loved pajamas, he or she still had to take the allotment of flannel shirts, and could not exchange them for another set of pajamas. And, if a child loved the color red, but hated green, then the woman in charge of *b'gdei yeladim* (children's clothes) would try to give the child his/her preference, but not "overdo" it, so as not to be seen to be favoring one child over another. If a child had received a present of clothes from a grandparent who lived outside the kib- butz; then he or she was given less *b'gdei Shabbat*, since fair was fair. *All* of the boys were given brown shoes and *all* of the girls were given red shoes. And, in order to really be sure that there was equality and that parental pressure was not brought to bear, as a rule, parents, or more specifically, mothers, were not al- lowed to accompany their children during their bi–annual trip to the *matpera* when they went to get their clothes–once for summer clothes and once for win- ter clothes. Helping pick out the clothes was the *mitapelet's* job.

But those were the good old days, and the kibbutz has changed since then. It has grown older, the *matpei'ra* is closed, since most of the members who worked there have either retired or have died and none took their place, and be- cause so many families left the kibbutz, reducing the need for a work branch that sewed children's clothing. The kibbutz has grown older, with a mean age of around sixty–five. The laughter and screams of the children no longer belong to *bnei meshek* ("children of the kibbutz") but rather to the children of the *to- shavim*. *Toshavim* are residents, who are not members, and who do not wish to become members. They come to live on the kibbutz for a few years, where they pay rent and pay for services so that they can enjoy quality of life. They send their children to *batei yeladim* that are, more often than not, run by hired *mi- taplot* from the development town, which is not far from the kibbutz. *Ha- chinuch hakibbutzi* now appears to mainly reflect the geographical location of the educational centers, and much less the ideological and educational values once taught.

As we walked, Natan commented: "It's so quiet here. Is it always so quiet now?"

Natan pointed out where his *kolelet* had been. *Kolelet* is a made-up kibbutz word which translates to something like "holder/container" or "community," but refers here to a child daycare center that included the formal classroom and the club house/recreation areas for after-school activities. He spent his elementary school years in that building, most of them not overly happy years. When Natan was in first and second grade, we were on *schlichut* in the United States to the Habonim Labor Zionist Youth Movement [*schlicut* literally means "mission" and connotes being on a mission for the Jewish/Israeli people]; *habonim* means "the builders," but is also the word for "beavers"–who are also builders, though not Jewish (or any other religion), as far as I know). In Chicago, where we lived during those years, Natan attended a Jewish day school where he learned to read and write in both Hebrew and English. Coming back to the kibbutz turned out to be a difficult experience, one that lasted throughout his high school years, as he realized more and more how he did not fit the mold that all *bnei meshek* were pressured, in both manifest and latent ways, to fit.

We continued on to the *tichon* (this usually means "high school"). On our kibbutz, *tichon* means "high school area" where children from the 10th grade on have their own *chevrat neurim* ("teen society"). The area includes a disco, club house, and dormitories. Natan pointed out the room where he had lived during those high school days, when he was often unhappy since he didn't/couldn't conform to the 'desired' image of the kibbutz high school adolescent, and, as a result, was too often bullied and victimized by his 'friends.'

I looked and listened for signs of melancholy as we walked around the *tichon*, but found none; he was happy to be back there, looking at his former home from the vantage point of an adult who feels good with the life that he has made for himself. I felt relieved that he no longer felt the pain of those *tichon* years, and that he could now look at it though different eyes. I felt relieved that David's and mine almost blind acceptance of the *chinuch hakibbutzi*, which had kept us from understanding the depths of Natan's unhappiness during those years and from working more actively to understand and help him, had not had disastrous results. I felt happy that his life has turned out so well, and that those years did not leave insurmountable scars in his gentle soul.

We came back toward home and I stopped in to find a disposable camera that I had bought a while ago so that I could take pictures as we continued on our walk. Natan laughed: "*Eema* (Mom)–you're acting like a tourist, taking pictures of everything on the kibbutz." "I kind of feel like one now–like I live here, but don't." As we continued on our walk, I took pictures of the gardens and of the tractors, of the cows and of the pub.

Across from the welding shop and garage, next to the gas pumps, there is a big sign, made from individual metal pieces and painted white, that says the name of our kibbutz. Next to the sign there is a metal sculpture of a sheaf of wheat. This stands on a small mound of dirt and is surrounded by grass and some bushes.

When they first put up the sign, somewhere in the mid 1990s, it was painted black. My first reaction was one of horror; it reminded me of the mass graves that I had seen in Bergen–Belsen. In that former death camp/now memorial, where the barracks had once stood, there are mass graves which were dug in order to incorporate all of the dead, due to the massive outbreak of typhus in that camp. When the British soldiers, who liberated the camp in mid April 1945, realized what they had found and the extent to which the disease had spread through the camp, they decided to burn down all of the buildings in attempts to stop the further spread of the disease and to create livable conditions. Not knowing the names of the incarcerated prisoners, and who was who, the people were buried in a number of mass graves (See The liberation of Bergen–Belsen: http://www.scrapbookpages.com/BergenBelsen/BergenBelsen05.html).

When I first visited the former death camp in 1989, I literally became paralyzed by the site. As I walked then through the pastoral park that had once been a place where Jews were sent to die of starvation and sickness, I saw mound after mound. On each one, there was a concrete inscription that said something along the lines of: Here are buried 10,000 people. Here are buried 5,000 people.

When the welding shop first put up that sculpture–sign, to welcome people to the kibbutz, I was horrified. To me, it looked like the mass graves I had seen there, in Germany. I was relieved when, a few years later, someone had the good sense to paint the sign white. I don't know if anyone else had the association that I had, or if they just decided that white looked more welcoming than black, but I began to see the sculpture–sign less as a grave, with its anonymous/ominous farewell, and more as a welcome to our little collective.

As we walked by the sign, I took a photo of Natan standing next to it. From there, we walked by the *refet*, where I took some more photos of cows, and continued on over to the *mo'adon tzi'irim* ("young adults' clubhouse; basically, a pub), where I took pictures of the motorcycle which is perched on top of a pole, welcoming *tzi'irim* ("young adults") from the kibbutz and from the area when they come on Friday night to hang out and relax after their week of school, army or work.

The pub reminded Natan that he had seen a childhood friend of his at lunch. Natan hadn't seen or spoken to him in many years, so when he saw him on the kibbutz, he was surprised that his friend was still around. Natan said: "I can't understand why *tzi'irim* stay here. Why do they want to stay? What do they get out of it?" There was no one answer that I could give him.

Being with Natan and walking around and *looking* at the kibbutz, I couldn't help but compare the old days with the new. For example, in the good old days, it was against the rules for a member to own a car. This would have gone against the principle of equality. All of the cars were kibbutz owned. If you wanted to go into Beer Sheva to see a movie, then you had to fill out a green slip with a request for a car at least two weeks ahead of time, and give it to the *sidron rechev* ("car manager"). It was important to get your request in early, for this was the only way to have the chance to actually make it to the movie (that might not have been playing anymore by the time you got a car). Today, we are much better organized and more up–to–date, and we have a computer program for this process. There is no need to order a car two weeks in advance; you can do so the morning or afternoon you want to travel and there is a fairly good chance that you will find an available car.

The rule forbidding private cars changed about 10 years ago, when people began buying cars without paying heed to the rule, and without asking for special permission to do so. *Va'adat chevra* (the community committee whose task was to prepare policy papers) then wrote a policy paper that laid out the guidelines for such purchases. Today, when you walk around the kibbutz, there are many cars parked along the side that belong to both *chaverim* and *toshavim*. If you did not know better, you might think that you are in a middle–class suburb, and not in a kibbutz.

Natan and I were winding up our walk when we passed an area on the road, located behind a neighborhood built in the mid 1980s and near the kibbutz cemetery that had been privately made into parking spaces. A log had been pulled over and painted red and white. On one part, painted in red, there was a sign written in neat block letters that said "private parking." Natan and I looked around and saw plenty of space to park. We stood there, staring at the "private parking space," wondering who had taken the trouble to make him/herself such a spot, and why he/she felt the need to do so. Was this spot better than the spot two meters from there? And, if for some reason, many people showed up to park in that area, and this meant that the person had to walk five meters to get to his/her house, was this a problem that needed such a solution?

The days of equality appear to be gone; children no longer get their clothes from the *matpeira* but buy them in the mall in Beer Sheva or in one of the outdoor markets in Tel Aviv. Some people have their own cars, with some even having their own private parking space. David and I each have a bicycle, and one of them usually has a flat. . . .

Chapter 6 or Planting olive trees with unrecognized Bedouins

One of the plans that I had for my time in Israel, during my semester off campus, was to participate in peace and social justice activities. I had the need to do something, and not just write about what I thought needed to be done, or comment on the work of others. I went to plant trees at *Al Sdeir* because I had the need to do something positive. I went to *Al Sdeir* because I felt that all I did was *talk* about the need for peace, and for social justice, but that it had been too long since I had done anything concrete to try to create the society that I thought would be better than the one we have. I also went to *Al Sdeir* out of curiosity; I wanted to see first-hand what a *k'far Bedoui lo mukar* (unrecognized Bedouin village) looked like, and how the people lived.

On Saturday morning, my good friend Tali, her mother–in–law, a *vatika* (old–timer) from our kibbutz, and I left our "legal" and "recognized" kibbutz, with our nice, clean warm houses, that have running water and electricity, to go to *Al Sdier* to plant trees. The *kfar* is approximately a 50 minute drive, yet a world away. You cannot find the village on a map. To reach the *kfar*, you need to drive to the southern exit of Beer Sheva. From there, you take the road toward Dimona. Approximately 5 minutes later, you turn left onto a one–way road which then turns into a dirt road, which winds around until you eventually reach the village–no more, really, than a collection of tin houses. It was a sunny and cold day, with some dark clouds in the sky that hinted at rain in the evening. I wondered how the villagers reached their home on a rainy day, when this dirt road would most certainly turn into a mudslide.

In the Negev (desert) region where I live, there are 45 unrecognized Bedouin villages. Since they are unrecognized by the Israeli government, they have no water, electricity, education, health, waste or other community services. These villages are comprised of tin houses that are put up by the community families (who are usually connected through kinship ties), and the villages are often surrounded by waste and garbage.

There are an estimated 80,000 people who live in these villages (see http://www. dukium.org for information and pictures). The Bedouin have set up these villages for a number of reasons–either because they have been pushed off of lands that they were on, do not want to settle in one of the "official" Bedouin townships, do not have where to settle, or because the village residents, who are usually families, want to stay together.

About two weeks before the tree planting, 50 families in this *kfra lo mukar* were served court orders that their homes were going to be demolished, since the houses in the unknown village had been constructed "illegally", without building permits (http://dukium.org/index.php). Unknown. . . Hmmm. . . . unknown to whom? The use of the term 'house' is very deceiving here; when one thinks of a house, an image of a permanent structure comes to mind. In *Al Sdeir*, the houses/shacks are made out of tin, and do not look as if they can serve as any kind of permanent home for a family for any length of time–certainly not in the heat of the summer or in the cold and rain of the Negev winter.

As a result of the court injunction, the Negev Coexistence Forum, or *Dukium* as it is known in Hebrew, together with other peace/social justice groups, held a tree planting day in *Al Sdeir*. *Dukium* decided to show solidarity with the villagers by creating life, instead of destroying it. The activity was called: Instead of House Demolitions, We are Planting Trees! (See http://dukium. org/modules.php?name=Topics). I was happy to have the opportunity to show solidarity and plant trees with approximately 150 people who showed up from the area, from Jerusalem and Tel Aviv to do the same.

Driving from the kibbutz to the meeting point for the participants who were coming from kibbutzim and cities and towns in the Negev took about 45 minutes. When we arrived at the Sara junction, there were six cars already there. People were standing outside, talking to one another, waiting for the arrival of the busses from Jerusalem and Tel Aviv. As I got out of the car, I was introduced to people from *Dukium* and was happy to see an old friend of mine, who had come to the activity with his wife and youngest daughter. Daniel, a former member of a kibbutz in my area, and I had studied together during our Masters programs. We had hit it off back then, in the beginning of the 1990s, and every time I was in Israel, we somehow managed to run in to one another and to "catch up." He has his doctorate in sociology, and his dissertation had looked at economic changes in kibbutzim. Daniel is one of those positive and sweet people that everyone likes and respects. As we waited for the other tree planters to arrive, we talked about my work at NSU, and he told me about his work at one of the local colleges, where he is on faculty.

Around 11:00, more cars and the busses arrived, so we all left in a convoy for *Al Sdeir*. Along the way, we saw a number of unrecognized villages–tin shacks with piles of garbage and waste, with waste and garbage scattered along the highway. When we arrived at the village, we were directed to a large tent that had been erected for the event. Colorful rugs and big pillows, most covered with white and embroidered pillow cases, were set out on either side. "How do they keep these so white?" Daniel asked me, and I had no answer. It was clear from the outset that only men from the village were to be our hosts; the women were nowhere in sight, and someone said that they were in their homes. The complete separation between Bedouin men and women, and the keeping of women from public and political gatherings in which men participate is not easy for a modern, Ashkenazi woman like me to accept. I wanted to be able to at least say hello to the women who were living in these tin houses that were to be destroyed soon. However, it did not seem the right time to mention this publicly. While this issue is often discussed in Jewish groups that work together with Bedouins, it has yet to be resolved.

We were served sweet tea and cookies and sweets by men and young boys. After Ariel, the Jewish Israeli coordinator of *Dukium*, gave a very short explanation about the place, using a bullhorn so that we all could hear, we broke into two groups to plant trees along the perimeter of the village. It was a lovely experience, planting trees with our Bedouin neighbors, though we all knew that the chance that these trees would survive was very slim, given that the villagers have little to no water and that they would not be able to divert this precious water for irrigation of the saplings. We were told by one of the men that their village was connected to a pipe, but that during the day there was no pressure, though it was somewhat better at night. When Tali's mother–in–law kept on asking if the trees would be watered, repeating that they couldn't live without water, the man said "Yes, at night." I didn't believe him; I think he didn't want to disappoint us that the trees were never going to see anything but rain water, and didn't want us to feel that all of our work was going to be for naught. It was rather a kind gesture on his part. The planting of the trees was more of a symbolic act than a concrete one–but we still all hoped that some of the young trees would make it.

One of the young men led my group to the southern perimeter. I asked him: "How many people live in this village?" He answered: "About 50 men." "And, how many people all together?" I had meant men, women and children, but it was clear from his answer that it was really only the men who mattered here, at least for him. "About 200–50 men and the rest are women and children." So, although three quarters of the villagers of *Al Sdeir* are women and children, they got lumped into one undifferentiated figure, while the 50 men were given double prominence.

We went over to the small truck to take saplings for planting. The young man showed us what the distance should be between trees, and then we noticed that there were no tools to dig holes. One hoe seemed to appear from nowhere, and within a few minutes, many more appeared. Tali dug a hole, and I planted the tree, then I dug a hole and an older Bedouin man planted another. We shared the hoes and the saplings, planting them in a haphazard way, much like the houses had been planted in the *kfar*. It took about one hour to plant two rows of olive trees along the southern perimeter of the *kfar*.

After the tree planting, we convened again in the tent, where we were served more tea and more sweets. We heard speeches by the heads of villages, who spoke about how the Bedouin have been denied their rights since the establishment of the State, in 1948, and how happy they were that Jews had come to hear their plea and to work together with them. The tree planters had also included two *Knesset* (Israeli Parliament) members–Talab El–Sana, a Bedouin from the Negev–from the United Arab List, and Chaim Oron–a kibbutznik from *Yachad* and the Democratic Choice (biographical information on *Knesset* members can be found at the official *Knesset* website: http://www.knesset.gov.il). Both of these men, one Jew and one Arab, one from a Zionist political party and one from an Arab, non–Zionist political party, spoke of the rights of every Israeli citizen to be entitled to running water, electricity, and education and health services. They spoke about the need of the government to enter into talks with the Bedouins, and not to continue with a policy of transferring Bedouins from one area to another, and uprooting of homes. One of the main organizers of the event was Atia al–Asem–the head of the Regional Council for the Unrecognized Villages in the Negev. He, along with heads of other unrecognized villages, also spoke of coexistence with the Jews and of the need for mutual respect for human and civil rights.

This was not your typical day in the Negev–where Bedouins and Jews meet in a Bedouin village, plant trees, and mingle with *Knesset* members and press from *Al Jazeera*.

On January 25th, Jews celebrated the holiday of *Tu b'Shevat*, which is the fifteenth day in the month of *Shevat* on the Jewish calendar. This holiday is the New Year of the Trees, one of the four new years during the year. This is a joyous holiday, one in which people go out and plant trees, celebrating and communing with nature. On our kibbutz, we have two traditions–one is called *meirutz hashtil* (the plant race) in which the children have a race around the kibbutz. The second tradition is the planting of trees around the kibbutz, which takes place after the children have finished the *meirutz* and received a certificate, with a picture of a tree, with the time that it took them to complete the run, and the date of the race. Since it usually rains around the holiday of *Tu b'Shevat,* the race and planting often have to be postponed by one week or two, when the roads and ground are not so wet and muddy.

For some reason, planting trees in a *kfar Bedoui lo muu-kar* does not inspire many Jews to come and commune with nature. What a pity, I think, for what is lovelier than a young tree taking root in the desert? If there is a God, I doubt whether She or He differentiates between the Negev of my kibbutz and the Negev of Al Sdeir.

Chapter 7 or Israel, the Holocaust, the survivors, and some of what comes between

As part of my desire to participate in as many lectures and seminars as I could while in Israel, I attended a seminar that was co–run by *Amcha*–the National Israeli Center for Psychosocial Support for Holocaust Survivors and the Second Generation (http://www.amcha.org) and Ben Gurion University. I was able to attend only the morning session of the seminar since I had made plans to meet Natan at the mall. The title of the day was: "Shoah testimonies: From the mouths of the survivors to the ears of the listeners." Every year, *Amcha* has such a seminar, one that brings together *nitzolim* (survivors) with researchers of the Holocaust.

I have often had problems with the term *nitzol*. *Nitzol* literally means "one who was saved." But I wonder–who did the saving here? Did the survivors make it through the war because somebody saved them, or because they somehow managed to hold on to life, often *in spite* of the fact that no one helped them? I have also never liked the word because it connotes that the survivors were passive ("were saved"). From the hundreds of survivor interviews that I have conducted or read, I have learned that most of the survivors made it through the war alive not because someone undertook actions that saved them from death at one point or another, though there are certainly such cases, but because they made a decision that fortunately turned out to be a correct one, concerning what they should or should not do, were lucky that they were not discovered, were mistakenly left for dead, and/or managed to hide their identity. Many of the survivors that I know do not like to be called *nitzolim*; they prefer the term *korbanot* (victims) or *sordim* (survivors–with an active connotation–*"Saradnu et hamilchama* or "We survived the war").

Whether they are called *nitzolim, korbanot* or *sordim*–they always come out in large numbers whenever there is a lecture, seminar or conference on the topic of the Holocaust or the survivors. *Amcha's* seminar day at the university was no exception.

The seminar was held in the auditorium in the Senate Building–a venue reserved for "serious" and "important" events, hence marking this seminar as one worthy of respect. Before I entered the auditorium, I stopped to have coffee and a *boreka* that were provided for the participants. This is the staple of BGU functions; I have yet to be at a conference at BGU where *borekas* were not served. I looked at the people who had arrived, noting to myself that the great majority were survivors. It is hard for me to explain *how* I knew that most were survivors, even those that I did not know, but I knew. I recognized some of the *nitzolim* as former interviewees of mine. Others looked familiar from previous Holocaust conferences and lectures.

When I walked into the auditorium, the people were greeting one another as they found seats: "Shalom! So, I see you've come." "Nu, what can I do? *Ani chavera b'mo'adon ha'ze"* ("I am a member of this club.")

The auditorium, with its wood paneling and comfortable swivel seats, is designed in the round; in front of each seat there is a personal microphone so that people in the audience can respond or ask questions during a meeting. The room is always semi–lit and quiet, giving it an aura of subdued seriousness. Even when all of the lights are lit, it is never bright. In spite of the signs that clearly say: "No food or drink allowed," a number of the participants had entered with coffee and a *boreka* or two. Israelis are notorious for ignoring signs in public buildings such as "No smoking," "No food or drink allowed," "No cellular phones." These signs always appear to me to be for some mysterious crowd whom I have yet to come across.

I sat down in the last row, facing the podium. An older man was sitting three chairs down to the left, and then a young man, who I assumed was a student, came and sat down next to him. The older man turned to him and said:

"Are you a son of survivors?"

Nothing like cutting right to the chase.

"No, my mother managed to immigrate in 1939 before the war. But most of her family was killed in the Holocaust."

And so much for warm-up and niceties, before getting into a deeper conversation.

"Why are you here? Does the topic of the Shoah interest you?"

"Yes, I'm a student and I'm writing a paper on the Shoah. It interests me." The young man took out a laptop from its case, and began setting it up.

The survivor and the student continued to talk, as if they had known each other for much longer than five minutes, when, quite randomly, they had chosen seats next to one another. As they talked, they realized that there were both from the same city. A few minutes into their conversation, the survivor opened up his briefcase and took out a page with crowded type that ran from the top to the bottom, single spaced. I heard him tell the student: "If you are interested in the topic–these are just the headlines. Behind each sentence is a whole story. Here, if you're interested, you can read it." The young man said "thank you" and began taking a cursory look at it. The *nitzol* continued: "I've been trying to write a book about my experiences, but I get too depressed. It's too much." Pointing to the text that he had given the son of a woman who had managed to escape from Europe in 1939 and settle in Palestine, he said: "behind each of these sentences is an entire story."

The old man then began to tell the student his wife's story, who was sitting to his left. She smiled, and nodded hello. She got up often to go outside, come back, sit down, and get up again. "Her family is from Germany. She was just a small child." He then went on again to say how he became so depressed when he tried to write his book; he was even admitted to the hospital not too long ago. "They thought it might be my heart; but it was my nerves."

The young man kept smiling, nodding his head, engaging the *nitzol* in further conversation. One might have thought that this young man was the *nitzol's* grandson; they appeared to know each other very well and they were discussing topics that might be considered very personal in a Northern American context. However, it did not strike me as odd that they were, in effect, strangers; this conversation was 'typically' Israeli in a way–it is not odd for an old man to engage a young one in stories of the past. This often happens on busses, or while waiting in line. The young man was carefully listening to the old man's stories of the Holocaust and his health, and showed no signs of uneasiness or discomfort. This is one of the beautiful sides of Israeli culture, I think.

Professor Avishai Braverman, who was the president of the university at the time, was invited to open up the proceedings. Braverman gave what I thought was a very strange speech. He began with apologizing for not being able to stay, since he had visitors from the US Defense department who were looking into collaboration with BGU. The only time that I remember Braverman staying for a seminar at BGU was when he participated in a post–Oslo seminar that focused on political and social life in Israel and Palestine, which took place after the collapse of the peace process. This conference had been attended by Ambassador Dennis Ross, who was the special Middle Eastern coordinator during the Clinton administration. I remember Braverman continually referring to Ross as "Dennis" and saying "I was just telling Dennis. . . ." It was clear then, and it was clear the day of the Holocaust seminar, that Professor Braverman feels comfortable among US visitors of power. I felt uneasy that the seminar on Holocaust testimonies began officially with an association to the US military and its connection to the university in the Negev.

Braverman went on to give what I call his "typical *spiel*"–the *spiel* (story) that he always gave at such meetings when he was president. He stated how BGU was in the process of opening up an Industrial Park, together with the regional authorities and how the northern train station, a kilometer away from the university, would be building a bridge to the university (how many years have I heard these claims?). He went on to say that, with these developments: "young people will come here to live and to work in quality employment." He also noted that 7,000 students currently live in Beer Sheva, and contribute to community life. Why did Braverman think that these points would be of particular interest to this audience comprised of *nitzolim*, a few students and academics? I wondered whether he ever wrote opening remarks that specifically related to the seminar he was addressing or if he did not see *this* particular seminar as being important enough to come up with something a bit more relevant.

As he reached the end of his remarks, he did mention the Holocaust; he told the story of his parents who had emigrated in 1936 from Europe and how most of his family had been killed in that genocide. He ended with the statement: "It has always bothered me that Israel suffers from superficiality and a lack of memory culture. There is ignorance about the past, and not knowing the past leads to a weak future. The Jewish people built here, in Zion, a country that has strength, but we have an internal problem of culture, morality and continuity." Again, making his apologies, since "the US military people are waiting for me," Braverman left.

The *nitzol* who was sitting a few chairs down to my left made a remark, in quite a loud voice, that this is what always happens. "The *important* people, who *need* to stay and listen, run away; *they* need to stay." It did not appear as if Braverman heard him. I could tell that the man was getting worked up, and that we would hear more from him as the day went on.

Dr. Bela Cantor, the head of the Beer Sheva branch of *Amcha*, opened up the seminar by talking about long–term effects of the Holocaust on the survivors that are not usually discussed. She recounted a story of raising the idea of opening up a *salon* on Polish literature in the Polish language in her *Amcha* branch. She was very surprised when the survivors from Poland, who she thought might be interested in such an activity, became very angry: "We've forgotten Polish because we don't want to remember it. We are angry at the Poles for not doing anything. We don't want to have any discussions in Polish." How tragic, said Bela, that in addition to all of the personal and collective losses, the *nitzolim* also lost their native languages. The story emphasized the continued feeling of alienation that survivors continue to feel to some extent, even after living for so many years in Israel.

Professor Hannah Yablonka spoke next. Yablonka is a world–renowned scholar of the Shoah who specializes in the history of the Holocaust and the survivors who settled in Israel, from the end of the 1940s through the 1960s, when most of the *nitzolim* immigrated to the country. She is also the daughter of *nitzolim*, as are many Holocaust scholars. It is interesting that many Holocaust scholars and clinicians who work with Holocaust victims and their descendants are either survivors themselves, or children of survivors. Examples include: Dori Laub, Robert Krell , Haim Dasberg, Zahava Solomon, to name just a few.

Before beginning her talk, she showed a clip from the Eichmann trial, which took place in 1961 in Jerusalem. The film showed Yehiel Dinur's testimony. Dinur–Israel's best known Holocaust author who went by the pen name of *Katzetnik* ("a concentration camp inmate"–KZ is the German acronym for Concentration Camp)–began giving his testimony, and then fainted in the middle. Most people who listened to the trial on the radio, or were present in the courtroom, remember Katzetnik's testimony as the most memorable moment of the Eichmann trial, not only because of the fainting episode, but also because it was during this testimony that *Katzetnik* spoke of "the planet Auschwitz," a term still widely used to describe the death camp.

Professor Yablonka used the film clip to talk about the social and cultural importance of *Katzetnik's* testimony, though, as she noted, from a legal standpoint, it was basically worthless and quite irrelevant given that it could not address specific accusations against Eichmann. She stated that although the testi monies of the survivors did not enter into the written report of the court findings (which was over 300 pages long), *no one* in Israel remembers or refers to the report, while *everyone* remembers the testimonies–especially that of *Katzetnik.* Yablonka asserted that the Eichmann trial was a turning point in that it transformed the Holocaust from a European and survivor problem into an Israeli issue.

Other speakers included Ofer Shiff, a historian who researches Holocaust memory books. His lecture focused on the question: do memory books tell the story of the Holocaust (that is, the macro and 'objective' level) or do they tell the story of the survivors (that is, the individual, and the 'subjective' level)? And, how can a historian, who attempts to get at the *insides*, the "facts" of the Holocaust, do so without being drawn into the subjective world of the *nitzolim*? Dr. Shiff said: "It is impossible to describe something that is indescribable. We can't touch something that cannot be touched."

The last speaker of the morning was Dr. Ilana Rosen, the head of the Rabb Center for Holocaust Studies at BGU. Rosen researches oral histories from "ordinary people" who survived the Shoah. She differentiated between the "cultural stories" of Primo Levi, Eli Wiesel, and Saul Friedlander (Friedlander's 1979 book *When Memory Comes* is a beautiful book of fragments, forgotten and recalled memories of the Holocaust, and issues of identity) and "ordinary stories"–the stories that "ordinary" survivors tell. Like Shiff, she noted the tension between the objective and the subjective recollections, noting that the boundary between the two is artificial, and often, blurred.

The talks were followed by a question and answer period began. As I thought, the *nitzol* who was sitting nearby, and who had exhibited signs of nervousness throughout the morning, could be quiet no longer. He opened with a cry: "Why are the survivors forsaken? Why don't they take care of them?" His voice broke and there were tears in his eyes, but he talked about the *nitzolim* in the third person, as if he were not one of them. There was an embarrassed hush in the room, and another participant was called on. After a few more questions were taken from the floor, all three speakers made some more short remarks. To their credit, all three professors–Yablonka, Shiff and Rosner–did not ignore the survivor, and attempted to give him some kind of answer. They said: "We hear your cry, you are not alone; we are listening." As the morning session ended, and people filed out for more borekas and coffee and juice, the survivor continued to talk to himself, and to a woman who came over to try and calm him down, with words and with a hug. The man continued to cry: "How many are left? The least they can do is take care of them!"

The *Shoah* is never out of the headlines in Israel. When you read through the daily papers, listen to the news on the radio, which is broadcasted at least every half hour, or watch the news on television, you will find at least one reference to the Holocaust. During the discussion of the disengagement from the Gaza Strip, it was in the headlines since the *mitnachalim* (Jewish settlers–those who have settled in the Occupied Territories), co–opted the Holocaust for their purposes. Men, women and children began wearing orange Jewish stars–

reminiscent of the yellow stars during the war–to show that they are victims, being forced from them home, and persecuted.

On our kibbutz, we have a few *nitzolim*. One of them was a child during the war, and hid in a Polish forest with his family. After the war ended, he, his brother and parents (amazing that they all made it through alive!) immigrated to North America. As a young man, he made *aliya* to Israel and to the kibbutz. *Aliya*–ascension or going up–is the term used when Jews immigrate to Israel. I made *aliya* when I was 19. People, who leave Israel to immigrate to other countries, are called *yordim*–that is, those who descend or go down. As can be seen, from the traditional Israeli perspective, *aliya* or *olim* (those who do the ascending) are looked at in a positive light, whereas *yirida*–going down and those who *yored* are seen in quite a negative light.

To return to my story, in the early spring of 2005, two articles connected to the *Shoah* were published in our kibbutz newsletter. The first one was about the mother of one of our members, who was hidden during the war by a Christian family in Holland. After the war, the mother established an organization that promoted dialogue between the two religions and set up a program in which Protestant University students learn about Judaism. She established two cathedras in Dutch universities and was awarded an honorary doctorate by one of them for her work. In addition to her work in Holland, the member's mother was also instrumental in establishing a *moshav* (a semi–collective rural community) called *Nes Amim* ("miracle of the people") in Northern Israel. This *moshav* brings together Christians and Jews for dialogue, and has brought together Palestinians and Israelis for the same goal. The article described the mother's work and celebration of her awards in Holland.

The second article was written by the man who had survived the *Shoah* by hiding in the forest with his family. Ze'ev's article, however, did not include personal memories of the Holocaust, but was an angry cry against the *mitnachalim* who usurped the term Holocaust for their own agenda. Ze'ev noted that he had been sympathetic toward the *mitnachalim*, to some extent. While, politically, he did not agree with Jews living over the *kav ha'yarok* ("the Green Line"), but as an observant Jew, he understood the religious connection to the land. However, their use of Holocaust terms and symbols had angered him so, as this misuse appeared to him to be a sacrilegious and a distorted adoption of symbols and meanings of the past. He called the *mitnachalim–polshim* ("invaders" or "trespassers") who have immorally stolen land from the Palestinians. Ze'ev referred to his own Holocaust past, to draw the connection between the 'correct' and the 'incorrect' use of the past in our daily political and social life.

I have to admit, I was surprised by this article. I never thought of Ze'ev as having these political views. I guess that it shows that even though you can live with someone in a small community for many years, you can still learn things about them that you did not know. I also learned that, once again, the Holocaust never leaves us, whether we are in Beer Sheva, Gaza, Holland or the kibbutz.

Chapter 8 or *Anachnu tzreechim l'daber* –We need to talk

After I had been back home for two months, the *mazkir* ("Secretary"–the term denotes the elected head of the kibbutz, whose job can likened somewhat to that of mayor) stopped me on the sidewalk, near the bus stop, as I was returning from our local store. *"Anachnu tzreechim ldaber"* ("We need to talk"). For me, these are three of the most frightening words in the Hebrew language, at least when it comes to the *mazkir* approaching a *chaver*. Yossi asked me to call him later and set up an appointment. I answered: "No problem." I was such a liar. On the phone, we decided that Wednesday would work out for both of us.

When I saw David later that day, I told him that Yossi wanted to talk to me, but didn't know why. The only thing I could think of was that he wanted to discuss financial arrangements, though I was unaware of any payments in which I was remiss, or, to be more specific, that there were any payments that I was supposed to be making to the kibbutz. But, who knows, perhaps there was some kibbutz rule of which I was unaware concerning what a *chaver* who is on *sh'nat chofesh* owes (in kibbutz terms, *sh'nat chofesh* translates to "a year off."). When a *chaver(a)* takes a *sh'nat chofesh,* he/she retains *chave-rut* ("membership"), but has no rights. That is, the *chaver* receives no budget, voting privileges are suspended, s/he cannot be a member of a committee, cannot use a kibbutz car, etc. In short, the kibbutz has no responsibility for the *chaver* during that period. I thought that perhaps Yossi wanted to talk to me about my plans, given that I was back living on the kibbutz for four months.

I hate when the *mazkir* gives me a cryptic messages such as: *"Anachnu tzree-chim l'daber"*–without telling me about what. I feel the dread in the pit of my stomach.

I have had some bad experiences in conversations with the *mazkir*. The first bad experience I had was in the summer of 1973, before David and I got married and before I was a *me'umedet* ("candidate"–here, it means a candidate for kibbutz membership). I had finished a year of studies at the Hebrew University and had come to the kibbutz to be with David before our wedding. At that time, my status was defined as "David's girlfriend."

Our wedding was set for August 21st–a date that was significant to us for two reasons: (1) It was my older sister's birthday; and (2) In 1940, on that day, Trotsky, who was living in Mexico, was killed by a Soviet assassin, who split his skull open with an ice pick (Moynahan, 1994). (Well, actually, it was on August 20th, but perhaps the news didn't reach Israel until August 21st, which is 7 hours ahead of time from Mexico.) It didn't surprise me that David would know such a fact–he had been a Russian history major in college–but I was surprised when one of the *chaverot* on the kibbutz, a woman who I did not associate with having knowledge of Communist history, also mentioned this fact one day when I was in the *matpe'ra* (laundry) picking up our clean clothes (on the kibbutz, we have a communal laundry that washes and folds members' clothes). I began to feel that I was getting married on a very important day.

Given that the wedding was still two months off, and that I had not 'officially' arrived on the kibbutz, I was surprised when the *mazkir* asked me to come talk to him. Yossi was also the *mazkir* back then–when he was much younger and in better health than he is today. I was 20 years old at the time, and naïve in the ways in which things were handled in the kibbutz. It did not occur to me to ask David to go with me to that meeting, and I guess that we both thought that Yossi just wanted some kind of "get acquainted" meeting.

I don't remember the details from that meeting, but I remember the terrible feeling that I had when I left, and how much I cried when I got back to our tiny room that was our home at the time. I think that Yossi probably asked me a bit about myself, and about the wedding arrangements, and then he told me that I would not be able to take off work for as many days as I had planned before the wedding, when my mother and sister came to visit. I remember being in shock at this news. I told Yossi that I wasn't officially on the kibbutz yet, that my belongings were still in my dorm room at the Hebrew University, that my mother had never been outside the United States before and was coming halfway around the world for the first wedding of one of her children, and that we had made numerous travel plans. All of this fell on deaf ears. I don't remember what the summary of the meeting was, other than my tears, but I do remember leaving Yossi's office feeling that I had made a grave mistake by deciding to come live at this particular kibbutz.

When I later told David about our conversation, David tried to calm me down and told me that things would be okay. But he also said that he understood why Yossi had called me in for a meeting, since, as *mazkir*, it was his job to see that the kibbutz was functioning correctly and that *chaverim* were following the rules. I remember reminding David that I wasn't even a *me'umedet*, let alone a *chavera,* and feeling somewhat betrayed and hurt by David that he didn't completely take my side.

My first encounter with the *mazkir*, before I had any official status at the kibbutz, was a bad one.

A number of years later I had another difficult conversation with the *mazkir.* Once again, it was Yossi. While, according to kibbutz ideology, the position of *mazkir* is supposed to be a rotating one (rotation, or *rotatzia* in Hebrew, is one of the principles of kibbutz life–it is supposed to help ensure equality among members and do away with the *Animal Farm* phenomenon), in reality there has tended to be a fairly small pool of 'suitable' candidates for the job, and so there are some *chaverim* who have held this position more than once. This is also true of the positions of *merekez meshek* (economic director) and, to a lesser extent, *gizbar* (treasurer). Unlike the positions of *merekez meshek* and *gizbar*, which have exclusively been held by men (see chapter 4), there have been women *mazkirot*. Traditionally, the position of *mazkir* has never enjoyed the same status level of the economically defined positions; perhaps that is one of the reasons that some *chaverot* have held the job.

In the end of the 1980s, I had another difficult discussion with the *mazkir*, but for a completely different reason than the first time, though it did involve my mother once again. This time, the conversation also included my younger sister, Mika, who was living on the kibbutz, at that time. Mika had come to visit me in 1974, fell in love with a kibbutz member, stayed for the birth of Natan, and then got married, become a member and had three children of her own. The reason that we went to speak to Yossi was because our mother, who was living in Detroit, had been diagnosed with breast cancer. We needed to go and be with her during the operation and see how her recovery went. Since we did not know how serious it was, and how long recovery would take, we came to tell the *mazkir* that both of us would need to be gone for awhile, and that we could not say exactly how long that while would be. The reason that we had to have this conversation with the *mazkir*, as opposed to just with the *sidran avodah* (work organizer), was because part of the *mazkir's* job was to take care of *chaverim's* problems, and our mother's illness definitely fell into the category of a problem.

Mika and I explained what had happened to our mother, and then told him that we were making arrangements to go be with her. We stressed that we were not asking for money for the trip from the kibbutz. As kibbutz members, we did not have the sums needed for an overseas trip and so our stepfather was going to pay for the plane tickets. However, we asked if the rides to and from the airport could be on the kibbutz expense, as opposed to our private expense, and we also asked that the kibbutz pay for some overseas phone calls that we needed to make. Yossi expressed his concern for our mother and wished her well. Then the conversation took a turn that we had neither expected nor welcomed.

Yossi asked why we *both* had to go. Couldn't just one of us go and the other stay since my mother would have someone to take care of her? I remember being shocked at the question. No, we told him. We both needed to go since she was the mother of both of us. Both of us were worried, nobody knew how bad things were, and we both needed to be with her and our family during her illness, operation, and recovery.

Then Yossi said something that I never expected to hear from the *mazkir* of my kibbutz, where I had been a member for over 15 years at the time, or for that matter, from any *mazkir* from any *kibbutz*. Yossi told us that we could both go– we weren't asking his permission, but we let that pass–but that we needed to understand that if our mother recovered, and then became ill again, and, heaven forbid, even died, the kibbutz would not be able to fund a trip for us, and that we both might not be given the time off that we would need for that second trip. I have no memory of what Mika or I said, but I do recall that I realized that the *mazkir* of my kibbutz was never going to be somebody to whom I could turn to for help. This was one of my major crises/breaks with the kibbutz.

My mother recovered from her first bout with cancer, and our trip to America lasted only about three weeks. The cancer came back about a year and a half later, and again, we went back to the States to visit her. This time, I do not recall even letting the *mazkir* know, and I cannot remember who the *mazkir* was at the time. My mother managed to make one last trip to Israel to visit with us. I have some wonderful pictures of her with Daniel, Noa and Natan. My mother, who had been a children's librarian and then a head of a small city library, loved to read to them and they loved it when she did.

In April, 1990, on *erev Pesach* (the first night of Passover–the night of the *seder*), I received a phone call from my brother, Gary, who had never called me in Israel before. At first I was excited, and thought that he was calling to wish us a happy holiday. Then I realized that something was terribly wrong. He called to let me know that mom had died the night before, in her sleep. They thought that it was heart failure, but wouldn't know for sure for awhile. I had to tell Mika the news. We made immediate arrangements to go, a difficult thing to do on *erev Pesach* when the entire country is shut down.

Mika and I did not ask permission from the *mazkir* nor did we ask for financial aid to go to our mother's funeral. Perhaps the kibbutz paid for the rides to and from the airport; I do not remember.

The next difficult discussion that I had with the *mazkir* was in 1990, when Eitan held this job. One of the reasons that this discussion was so difficult was because Eitan was a good friend of ours, and so I had expectations that he would handle the issue that I brought to him and the *mazkirut* in a sensitive fashion. The *mazkirut* was the main kibbutz committee, headed by the *mazkir,* which was in charge of discussing all major kibbutz personal and community issues. The *mazkirut* no longer exists, but has been replaced by what is now called *ha-hanhala hachevrateet* (the social directorate). I have yet to understand the difference between the two and why the change was needed. I see the change as being one that was to bring the *mazkirut* a higher level of status by calling it a directorate. But, this assumption and analysis may be wrong.

I had been accepted into the Master's psychology program at BGU, not a small accomplishment, since the department only accepted five students each year out of approximately 10 times that number of candidates. I came to the *mazkir* to ask permission to continue on to a Masters degree. On the kibbutz, it was accepted practice to earn a Bachelor's degree, and the kibbutz paid for its members to do so, giving them tuition, money for books and expenses, and giving them time off from work to complete their studies. However, graduate degrees were basically unheard of and the few members who had obtained their graduate degrees, up to that point, only men, if I recall correctly, had done so because they were *ovdei chutz* ("outside workers"–the term for people who work off the kibbutz and deposit their salary into the communal kibbutz bank account. When I was a lecturer at the university, I did this as an *ovedet chutz*.) These men were able to obtain their graduate degrees because they worked in jobs that allowed them to also go to school and they received scholarships from the universities. This meant that they needed neither time off from work nor financial help to go to school. My request for the kibbutz to allow me to go on for my Masters was the first request of its kind. I was not asking for money, since I had a scholarship, but for permission to take some time off work to pursue the studies.

I had a discussion with Eitan and explained the situation to him–that I had been encouraged by my mentors to apply, had done so and had been accepted. I told him that if I did not begin my studies that year, I would forfeit my place and need to reapply the next year, with no guarantee that I would be chosen again. *Ya'ani* ("that is"), if I didn't go to school that year, then I would most likely be saying *shalom* to graduate school. I further explained to Eitan that the reason that I hadn't brought my request to *Va'adat limudim* ("the Study Committee" that decided who would get to attend university) was because all of this had happened after the *va'ada* had made its decisions and they had already allotted all of the spaces.

Eitan told me that he would bring my special request to the *mazkirut* for discussion. I waited to receive an invitation to come to the meeting and present my case, but never got one. Instead, a few days later, I received a summary of the *mazkirut's* decision which stated that my request had been denied. I was also informed, on the same piece of paper, that an appointment had been set up for me to come to their next meeting to appeal the decision.

Another unpleasant surprise. No invitation, no chance to explain directly what I was asking for, and a built–in appeals process that demonstrated that the *mazkirut* knew that I wasn't going to be happy with their decision. I thought to myself: why didn't they save us all of the heartache and trouble and just invite me the first time so that I could explain the request? Why were kibbutz bureaucracy and management always so backwards?

My appeal to the *mazkirut* was accepted and put to a vote in the *asepha* (the general assembly–the *asepha* is comprised of all kibbutz members and was the forum where kibbutz decisions were taken.) We used to have *asephot* every week, then every two weeks, then once a month until this system, which was no longer working, due to the apathy of the *chaverim,* was replaced by the *moetza* (council). There my request was granted and I entered the Masters program in psychology.

When I completed my Masters, I was smarter than I had been before (at least in the fields of organizational and social psychology, but hopefully also in the ways of kibbutz) and applied for the PhD program without asking anything of the kibbutz. I obtained a full scholarship–which included a stipend and salary for teaching–and continued on with my studies without asking for any 'favors' from any of the kibbutz *va'adot.* While this strategy was not exactly *kosher*, it worked since everybody benefited from it: I was able to pursue my doctorate and the kibbutz received a salary for my work.

The last two conversations that I had with the *mazkir*–once again, who happened to be Yossi–were not unpleasant, though the meetings in the *hanhala chevrateet* were. I went to Yossi to ask for a *sh'nat chofesh* after I had accepted a faculty position at NSU. I explained how I had not secured a position at one of the Israeli universities and that I needed to take this job that would, hopefully, further my academic career. Perhaps it was because Yossi had gotten older and was not in the best of health, or perhaps for other reasons, Yossi was very friendly and helpful, and tried to help David and me come up with a plan that would combine the idea of a *sh'nat chofesh* with that of *avodat chutz*. He invited us to the *mazkirut* to present our request.

David and I went home and discussed the possibilities. Neither of us was confident that such a 'creative' response would be successful, but we decided to give it a try. We came up with the idea that the kibbutz would continue to pay my medical coverage and social security and put money into my pension fund while teaching at NSU, but that I would not receive a *takziv* (budget) from the kibbutz and that I would cover all of my expenses while living in Florida. We also decided that each month I would send the kibbutz approximately $400 as salary for my work. In this way, I would retain all my rights as a *chavera,* but would not be a burden on the kibbutz. We also decided that we would not fight for this suggestion; if we sensed that the *va'ada* members were opposed to this unconventional approach, we would go back to requesting a *sh'nat chofesh*–a status that everyone understood.

During the first meeting in June 2003, my request for a *sh'nat chofesh* was accepted, but my suggestion that the year might be considered *avodat chutz* in Florida was rejected out of hand. I remember one of the *va'ada* members saying: "This is a 'creative' solution. We don't want 'creative' members here." Some of the other members smiled in agreement. It was clear that creativity and thinking in non–conventional kibbutz ways remains an unwanted trait for a *chaver(a)* to exhibit. I took the *sh'nat chofesh* and said *toda raba* (thank you very much).

I did not bring up the suggestion again for *avodat chutz* in the US when I reapplied for a second *sh'nat chofesh* in August 2004. This time I knew that it would be more difficult for the *hanhala hachevrateet* to grant this request, since this was actually going to be my third *sh'nat chofesh*–I had taken one during 2001–2002 when I had a post–doctorate at the University of Missouri in St. Louis. I came prepared for the worst. Once again, I saw the same drawn faces, the same embarrassed looks. It was clear to me that the *chaverim* on the committee did not know what to do with me–how many times can they grant unconventional wishes to a *chavera* who refuses to do what everyone else is doing?

Yossi was supportive, once again, and opened up the discussion, after I explained why I was asking for another year to work in the university in the US. While there was one member who staunchly supported me, and even brought up the idea that this should be considered *avodat chutz* and not a *sh'nat chofesh,* it was clear that the others were not in agreement. The *chavera* in charge of Human Resources, who has a high school diploma, but never went on to study after she graduated high school over 30 years ago, or has any idea what it means to have an academic career, told me:

You know, you can't always get what you want. You want a job in
the university, but sometimes things don't work out. You're going to
have to change your plans. You can't always get what you want. If you
can't find a job, and you come back to the kibbutz, I will help you find
one.

Yes–I was definitely going to depend on the *chavera* who had never seen
the need to extend her education after high school to find me a job. It was as if
she was telling me that I had wanted to buy a pair of blue pants, but they only
had black, so I needed to make due with the black pair. In my eyes, she had re-
duced an academic career to buying a pair of pants.

Anachnu tz'reechim l'daber–We need to talk. I can't wait for the next conversation with the *mazkir.*

Chapter 9 or My soldiers, the Palmach and invisible enemies

Tz'ahal (the acronym for *Tz'va Hagana L'Yis'rael*–the Israel Defense Forces) and *chai'yalim* (soldiers) are an everyday part of Israelis' lives. When I first came to the country, most likely like everyone else who first arrives, I was struck by the number of soldiers on street corners, in bus stations, in restaurants, in shops. I was struck by the sea of rifles, and by the presence of military equipment on the roads. I remember being overwhelmed at how many soldiers there appeared to be, how so many of them appeared to know one another, and how they seemed to take over every bus that I was on.

When I first came to the country, the soldiers looked mature, but that was probably because I was not quite 18 years old myself, and they were just a bit older than I was. Today the *sadirnikim* (soldiers in *sadir*–the regular army in which the men serve for three years and the women serve for two years of compulsory service) look so young. They *definitely* are too young to be involved in the bloody wars that have been going on since late September 2000 in Palestine and the one that took place in Lebanon this last summer.

I have a memory involving a soldier, from my first day in Israel, when I arrived with my group for the Workshop program in September of 1970: At the airport, we boarded a chartered bus to drive down to the kibbutz where we would be living for the year. We stopped in Beer Sheva, along the way, to have some lunch. On our way out of the restaurant, a soldier asked our bus driver where we were going. When he told him that we were headed toward the south, the soldier asked for a lift, which, of course, the driver agreed to. That was in the good old days when soldiers often hitched rides and people often gave them rides; I'm not sure that today a bus driver of a chartered bus would agree to give a soldier a lift.

We drove along the Arava road, which is the main road that leads down to the southern part of the country. This road cuts through the desert, and was in the middle of nowhere, or at least that is how it seemed to me. The soldier rang the bell, the bus driver pulled over, and the soldier got out and began walking across the desert. We all stared at him. Where was he going? How did he know when to ring for his stop? Wasn't he going to die of thirst wandering around in the middle of the desert, where it was clear that there was no settlement? I remember our *madrich* (counselor) from the kibbutz laughing and assuring us that the soldier would be fine.

This scene repeated itself over the year. Whenever I took a bus from Tel Aviv or Beer Sheva down to the kibbutz, there were always soldiers on the bus, and a few of them always rang the bell for what seemed to me to be imaginary stops along the way, in the middle of nowhere. They would get off the bus, and walk into the desert and I was never really sure that they would be heard from again. Of course, the soldiers knew where they were going, and the more adapt I became at making out signposts and seeing signs of military life, such as a few tents in the distance, I realized that those soldiers were not going to die in the middle of the desert.

My husband became a soldier before we got married. When I made *aliya* in 1972, David was three quarters through his service. Being 'old' (he had entered the IDF when he was 24 years old; most enter at the age of 18), he only had 9 months of military service, as opposed to the three years that the 18 year olds had. I returned from the Workshop program in July 1971 and David had been inducted in October of that year, so when I made *aliya* in the spring of 1972, I hadn't seen him since he had become a soldier. David had written to tell me that he would come to the airport to meet me when I arrived. He had been given a few days of vacation and so we would be able to spend my first few days in Israel together. After I finished with the formalities at the airport (I had arrived as a *toshevet ar'ai'eet* [temporary resident] so I needed to get my *te'udat oleh* [immigrant card] and undergo some other bureaucratic procedures as well) and collected my bags, I came out to meet my grandparents, who were living in Jerusalem at the time, and David, who were to be waiting for me.

I remember the first look that I got of David as a soldier–it took me a moment to recognize him. He looked like all of those other soldiers that I had seen during my year on Workshop! He had become one of *them*–one of the masses dressed in green, with a gun slung over his shoulder and a beret stuck in one of his epaulets. This was the first time that I had a direct connection to a soldier–*my* boyfriend was a soldier in the Israeli army! It was a strange feeling. It turned out that David's vacation had been cancelled. As David explained to me, it was, after all, the army, and their promises of leave always had to be taken with grains of salt. Instead, he had been given a few hours leave to meet me before he needed to make his way back to his base.

Of course, the strangeness of being connected to soldiers has dissipated over the years. Not only was David a soldier, but all of our male friends on the kibbutz were soldiers, as well as many of our female friends as well, back then in the early 1970s. My neighbors were soldiers, their children became soldiers, and now some of them are old enough to have grandchildren who are soldiers. I have known people who were killed, when they were soldiers. My children were/are soldiers.

After David finished his regular service, he did another 22 years of *mi'luim* (reserve duty) and was often gone for up to a month at a time, and more during the Yom Kippur War, when he was gone for nearly six months. This was not the best way to begin a marriage, nor was it the best way for me to begin my accli-mation into the kibbutz. I was always sure that the army had it in for me; other-wise, what could explain the army consistently, or so it seemed at the time, call-ing him to *mi'luim* during the holidays, when it is so important for family to be together? Even though everyone in my family, and almost everyone I know, has served in the army, I have never become completely accustomed to this–not really–at least not when it comes to my own children. I have never grown accus-tomed to seeing my children with their guns and I always feel uncomfortable when I come into the house, and see a rifle leaned up against the wall. They al-ways seem, somehow, not to be my children, when they are in uniform. This distance is frightening, and I wonder why I have never been able to completely accept this part of their (my) lives.

I have never thought of our family as being a "military" family. David hated almost all of his army service–both *sadir* and *mi'luim*–and he rarely talked at length about his army experiences, as many of our friends and acquaintances did. When he *did* talk about his experiences, his talk lacked the bravado that the others had; his stories were usually about how he had suffered because they didn't have what to eat, or where to sleep, or how cold it was, or just how terri-bly boring it all was. He never liked being called up for *mi'luim* and did not see it as a vacation from work or the family. He would become pretty miserable whenever he was in the service, or whenever he got a *tzav* (order or draft notice) to come to *mi'luim*. For that reason, he always hated checking if we had mail; he was afraid of finding a brown envelope, the color of the envelopes of the *tza'vim*. In that way, I always felt that we didn't quite fit into the "normal" Is-raeli culture.

After he completed nearly 22 years of service, in 1993, David received his *shichrur* (liberation–used to mean release/discharge) from army service. David and I went to the army headquarters in Tel Aviv, where he was given his release form and a certificate for his years of duty. I believe that this was the happiest day in David's life–more than our wedding day, and more than the birthdates of our children. I can understand and accept this.

I never served in the IDF. This was because I came to Israel at the age of 19 as a temporary resident and became a citizen three years later. By that time, I was already married, and the army did not draft married women, although they did, and still do, draft married men. At the time, I was extremely grateful that that was the case, since I could not imagine myself as a soldier. Indeed, I think that if I had thought that this was even a possibility, I would probably have post-poned my *aliya* for a few years. Over the years, in spite of my almost–but–not–quite pacifist views, I have regretted that I never had the experience. This is be-cause the army is *such* an integral part of Israeli society and culture, that I feel that by not having had the experience, there is some part of Israeli life that I will never be able to fully understand. I will never be really able to understand what the soldiers go through. I believe that it is not enough to know soldiers, to have children who are soldiers, and to be faced with the military every day of your life to know what it *means* to be a soldier.

I have always had what could best be described as a love–hate relationship with the army. I am fascinated by it, yet repulsed by it. I see *tzahal* as having made my life secure. This began as early as the Yom Kippur War or when the army would stop a suicide bomber from entering Israel. However, I also see the army as making my life less secure, and putting us all in danger, as in the case of the ongoing house demolitions, the uprooting of trees in Palestinian areas, and other violent acts carried out by IDF soldiers in the territories–thus leading, in my opinion, to reciprocal violence from the Palestinians. I am proud that all of my children were/are soldiers; I am angry that they had to be soldiers.

As part of this love–hate relationship, and my fascination with the army, soldiers, and modern Israeli history, I had wanted to visit *Beit Haplamach*–the *Palmach* house–in Tel Aviv, ever since it had opened in 2001. In January of 2005, when Natan was in Israel for a visit, I finally had the opportunity to do so.

David, Natan and I succeeded in joining in a group that had scheduled a visit *Beit Hapalmach*. It is still very difficult to obtain tickets to this museum/exhibit/show–it is hard to know exactly what to call it (see http://www.palmach.org.il). The museum only accepts groups of up to 25 people, and for many years, the waiting list to arrange a tour was six months. I had tried before to join a prearranged group, but had never succeeded. This time, I did.

We arrived at the museum, about 15 minutes before the tour was to begin. As we were waiting, a Jewish American woman came in with a group of 10 people, and I realized that this would be the group that we would be joining. I noticed that these were *dossim* (the not so polite slang word, taken from the Yiddish, for *dati'im*, which signifies observant Jews) and included some young and thirty–something aged adults, as well as a number of children. Another English speaker, who was on his own, also joined the group.

The cashier, a young man named Itai, who also turned out to be our guide, directed us to a bench where we could wait until the tour began. Itai encouraged us to look at the photo exhibit along the wall while we waited. David, Natan and I chatted and I also tried to hear what the Jewish–American–Israeli woman was saying, as she presented a history of Israel. She was holding a large book that contained photographs and maps. This woman had a 'teacher's' voice; she was pointing to the photos/maps, telling the history, and stopping to let the 'students' fill in the blanks: "In 1947, the UN came up with a partition plan for Palestine. And the Jews, who had been through the Holocaust, were happy to take anything, even if meant very little land, accepted the plan. And what did the Arabs say?" She looked at them, waiting for a response from her group. "No," a few answered. "Correct," she continued. "And then they attacked Israel."

Itai, who had made his way over to us, politely stopped the guide so that he could give us the official introduction and explain what we would be seeing, before we entered the exhibit. He spoke in a faltering, though clear English. Itai explained the background to the *Palmach* which is an acronym for *Plugot Machatz* (Striking forces)–the underground and commando unit of the *Hagana* (Defense)–the Jewish army. This army was established in Palestine, with the knowledge of the British, who then had the mandate for control of the country. Some of Israel's greatest leaders and heroes were in the *Palmach*. These included Yitzchak Rabin, Moshe Dayan and Yigal Allon, who was the commander of the *Palmach* (Bickerton & Klausner, 2001).

According to Itai, "the 1940s were the most dramatic decade for the Jewish people, at least in modern times" since this was the decade of the Holocaust and the decade in which the State of Israel was established. Itai explained, how during WWII, the Germans, led by Rommel, posed a real threat to the British and Palestine, by their offensive in Egypt (Segev, 1993). In expectation of war, the British allowed the Jews in Palestine to arm so that they would be able to help fight the enemy. However, once the German army was stopped at El Alamein, the British no longer 'needed' the Jewish soldiers and demanded that they disarm and disband. This is when the *Palmach*, which had been established in 1941, went underground (www.palmach.org.il).

Itai went on to talk about the guerilla warfare used by the *Palmach* against the British, in attempts to 'convince' them to leave Palestine. However, in order to succeed at this, they needed weapons, and in order to purchase these–via Jews abroad who helped smuggle them into the country–they needed money. These goals were accomplished when *Palmach* members moved to kibbutzim where they made arrangements to work for half a month and train for the other half.

The *Palmach* was not alone in its fight against the British forces; the forces coordinated actions with two other underground armed units–the *Lehi* (an acronym for *Lochemi Herut Yisrael*–Fighters for the freedom of Israel)–and *Etzel* (an acronym for *Irgun Tzva'i Le'eumi*–The National Military Organization (see the following website for information on these paramilitary organizations: http://www.jewishvirtuallibrary.org/jsource/History/lehi.html). While the *Palmach* has always been considered, by mainstream Israeli society, to have been a legitimate armed unit–since it was the precursor to the IDF–the *Lehi* and *Etzel* did not really enjoy legitimation; they were viewed not only by the Arabs and the British as terrorists, but by many Jewish Israelis as well.

The *Palmach* had a number of missions: they helped smuggle Jewish refugees into the country, mostly from Europe, after the Holocaust. The movie *Exodus,* tells the story of a *ha'pala* (venture or daring–the word used for the illegal immigration of Jews to Palestine during the British mandate); they destroyed British equipment, strongholds and installations; and they created new settlements. We learned in the exhibit, that throughout its years of existence, there were 7,000 members of the *Palmach*. Of these, there were 1,135 casualties–16% of the entire force.

One day after the UN voted to partition Palestine into two states, one Jewish state and one Arab state, the Arabs, who had rejected the partition plan, attacked the new Jewish state. This is the war the Israelis call the War of Independence and the Arabs call *Al Nakba*, or the Catastrophe (Bickerton & Klausner, 2001). The *Palmach* led the war, until it merged with the other units when the IDF was created in 1948 (see the Israel Defense Forces website at www.idf.il). The *Palmach* had three brigades–*Yiftach* in the North, *Har'el* in Jerusalem, and

Hanegev, in the Negev. In high school, children in learn a great deal about the battles fought by these brigades, and often take class trips to follow the battles' routes.

Beit Hapalmach has 12 rooms. Each room, except for the first one, which is a memorial for the fallen, is designed to represent a different locale in which the forces lived and fought. For example, one room is designed to look like the desert, where the *Palmachnikim* often trained; another looks like a forest, where the young soldiers would sit around a campfire, singing songs–such as *Shir Hapalmach* (the *Palmach* anthem)–and tell *chizbatim* (slang for 'cock and bull stories'). A third room is designed as one of the ships on which *ma'apilim* came to Palestine, after the Holocaust. There are no typical museum exhibits in these rooms; rather there is a docudrama film that continues from room to room in which we meet seven 'ordinary' *Palmachnikim*. We follow their story from their first day of recruitment in 1941 to after establishment of the State in 1950. We are witnesses to soldiers who fall in love; we see some fall in battle; we see another wounded for life.

The movie is very melodramatic and works on emotions. I had come to the museum with a critical eye; I had heard about the 'Disney' like effects from others who had visited before, and I was quite cynical about what I would see. I also understood that the museum showed a very narrow perspective of that period in Israeli history, not taking into account any other view but that of the *Palmachnikim* and the official Israeli account of those historical events. I watched the film, followed the characters, and realized that I was becoming attached to them. I shed a slight tear when they faced tragedy. It sucked me in, perhaps not as much as some others, but the museum worked its magic.

If you didn't know that the *Palmach* was first formed to fight the British, and then continued on to fight the Arabs, you might get the impression that this was an organization of young Jews who learned how to work and fight, suffered losses, and fell in love, but had no concrete enemy. The British were mentioned a few times, but except for a few blurry black and white pictures in newsreels from the period, there was no portrayal of a British soldier in the movie. And the Arabs were mentioned no more than three times–and I only noted two photographs of them. Who were the *Palmachnikim* fighting? How did the 1,135 soldiers fall, when their enemies were invisible?

The movie/exhibit ends when one of the *Palmachnikim* reads verses from the poem, *Silver Platter,* which was written by one of Israel's major poets, Natan Alterman, over the grave of one of their friends who fell in battle. This poem is about the young *Palmachnikim*–the young Jewish men and women who sacrificed their lives so that we, Israelis, could have a country. I entered *Beit Hapalmach* with a cynical outlook, and left with a slightly less cynical feeling. I came ready to scoff at the exhibit, and left feeling somewhat touched by and in awe of what I had seen and learned.

Old emotional and ideological ties die hard. I know that not all *Palmachnikim* were as sweet, innocent and dedicated as the characters in the film. The massacre of innocent civilians at Dir Yassin (Pail & Isseroff, 1998) was carried out, in part, by real members of the *Palmach*, not by fictional characters. With this, I know that if the *Palmach* and the *Haganah* had not been successful, there would have been no Israel.

I have a love–hate relationship with the army and with the history of modern day Israel. I hate the army and the violence that has spilled over from our militaristic society and culture into our everyday lives. I love the army for keeping us safe. I hate the soldiers who humiliate and abuse Palestinian citizens (Breaking the Silence–http://www.shovrimshtika.org presents some of these testimonies). But, I can't hate the soldiers, because I have known and loved so many of them, and one of them is now mine.

Chapter 10 or "It's principle"–*Anachnu tzr'ichim l'daber*–Take 2

At the end of January, I had that dreaded conversation with the *mazkir* (see chapter 8). Yossi called me at 11:30 and asked if I could come over to meet with him. I wasn't doing anything special, so I said yes and rode over on my bicycle to his office.

The *mazkir's* office is an old *tzrif* (wood hut/shack), that was built during the 1950s. Most of the *tzrifim* were taken down during the 1980s, but a few still stand, perhaps, in part, to remind us of roots, as it were. The only other *tzrif*, which is still standing, houses a small jewelry workshop. The jeweler makes beautiful silver and gold earrings, rings, brooches and necklaces, some with precious stones that are very popular with visitors and with *chaverim* looking for gifts to buy. Most of the original *tzrif* in which the *mazkir's* office is located was torn down quite a while ago. It used to serve as a classroom and had a public bathroom and shower as well–one that I used when I first came to the kibbutz and lived in a room that did not have a bathroom. The part which was left standing, which is the *mazkir's* office, is pretty similar to the way it was when it was first built. The outside of the building was painted yellow a number of years ago, the floor was also redone, and a small air conditioner was installed, but I doubt if anyone remembers when.

Around 15 years ago, the *mazkira* (feminine for *mazkir*), who was a clinical psychologist by training, brought in some 'comfortable' chairs so that when a *chaver(a)* came to talk about a sensitive issue, s/he wouldn't have to sit at the table and face the *mazkira* at her desk, like in a "formal" meeting. When the *mazkira* finished her term of office, she left the chairs for her successors. And while the chairs have remained throughout the changing of the *mazkirim* over the last decade and a half, I doubt that the burnt orange pillow covers have ever been laundered. The only other attempt to make the office appear more 'modern' or cared for are the salmon/pink Venetian blinds for the windows that were also purchased sometime during the decade of the 1990s. I have never seen these blinds raised; I suppose this is to afford privacy to the *chaverim* who come to talk to the *mazkir*.

When you enter the *tzrif*, which is basically one rectangular room, the 'comfortable' chairs are by the door, and then immediately there is an oblong table with a brown Formica top that is supposed to look like wood. The table is surrounded by simple chairs, gathered together from different periods and places, probably enough for all of the members of the *hanhala hachevratit* (the community directorate) that meets in the *mazkir's* office once a week to discuss the major social issues of the kibbutz. Along the long side wall of the *tzrif* is a white board. It seems to me that what is written on the board has been there for years (a list of budgets and their figures). Every time that I have been in the *mazkir's* office during the last two years, I have noticed this list. Given that I haven't seen a change (no additions or subtractions to the board), it does not seem that this board gets much use, or is even noticed by the *mazkir* or by his *hanhala*. Pushed up against the long table (which never looks like it has been dusted) is the *mazkir's* desk, piled with numerous stacks of papers. Behind this desk, along the back wall, there is a computer, printer and fax, and low shelves, holding folders and loose leafs. I wondered whether Yossi ever used the computer, or if he knows how, and I also wondered what kind of faxes he received in his office–were they secretive in nature?

There is one little offshoot from the main room. When facing the *mazkir,* to the left, there is a tiny 'kitchen' that has a sink, refrigerator, and a place to make coffee and tea. In this niche there are more shelves with files and binders and extra chairs that can be pulled out and used, if a large meeting is being held.

Yossi was on the phone when I came in; with his hand he motioned for me to sit down across from him to his right. I had no idea who was on the other end of the phone, but it became clear that he was talking about one of the *chaverim,* who is has a physical problem, and was explaining to the person about technical arrangements that were being made for this *chaver* at his work place. Since "this is kibbutz," I wasn't really surprised that Yossi was conveying potentially confidential matters about one of the *chaverim* to someone else while I was in the room; however, I was uncomfortable being present at such a conversation and thought, that if he had been talking about me, I would not appreciate him doing so in front of another *chaver* who was waiting to have a discussion with him.

After Yossi finished on the phone, he turned to me and smiled and asked *"Ma nishma?"* ("What's up?") I told him that all was fine. He then asked me "What are your plans?" I told him that I didn't have plans, but I could tell him what I was already doing. He nodded for me to continue. I then told Yossi that I had succeeded in obtaining a semester off campus and that I was teaching online classes for Nova, working on research and being with my family.

Then the other shoe (from chapter 8) dropped.

"There's a problem," Yossi said. He told me that since I was on *sh'nat chofesh*, I could not live on the kibbutz for such an extended time. *Sh'nat chofesh,* Yossi explained, is a year when the *chaver mitnatek* (disengages or removes him/herself, but can also mean breaks) from the kibbutz. He said that if I were to come for a visit of 10 days or two weeks, nobody would mind. He said, "We would let it pass." But, he could not overlook four months. He could not say "I didn't know that Julia was here for that long."

I asked Yossi what the problem was–was this a financial issue? That is, was Yossi telling me that I needed to pay rent for living on the kibbutz while on *sh'nat chofesh?* "It's a financial issue, but not *only* a financial issue; it's a matter of principle." Yossi reiterated that when a member who takes a *sh'nat chofesh* from the kibbutz, he or she decides to try life out somewhere else, and that somewhere else, by default, cannot be the kibbutz. Now, Yossi said, he understood that my case was special, different from most cases. I had taken a job in the US and now that I was on sabbatical, I wanted to be with my family. But, still, rules are rules and *ekronot* (principles) are *ekronot*. And so Yossi turned to me and asked: "So, what do we do? Do you have an idea?"

I told Yossi that I had no suggestion, since it had never occurred to me that I wasn't allowed to be on the kibbutz. When I had brought up the possibility of being home for a semester, before I went out on my last *sh'nat chofesh,* no one had mentioned that this might be a problem. I had not tried to hide the fact that this was what I was trying to do; in fact, I had mentioned it quite clearly in all of my conversations with him and with the *hanhala hachevratit.* I had brought it up since, at the time, I was half-heartedly trying to convince the committee members that my work at NSU would not be considered a *sh'nat chofesh,* but rather *ovadat chutz* (outside work). This idea was immediately dismissed by the members of the *hanhala hachvratit.* Yossi agreed that I had mentioned this as a possibility before, and that he did not think I was trying to hide anything, but that *then* it was a hypothetical issue, and *now* it was fact. And it was a fact that we needed to deal with.

I asked Yossi if he had a suggestion. He looked at me and laughed a bit: "No, I was hoping you would have one." He told me to think about it, to talk to David and to see if we could come up with an idea that could be agreed upon by all sides. "I don't want to force you into any decision that you don't want." However, after saying that, once again, Yossi explained that a *chaver* on *sh'nat chofesh* cannot live on the kibbutz. "Ten days to two weeks–we can let that pass –but four months? We need to make an arrangement."

Before our conversation ended, Yossi felt the need to explain to me why my staying on the kibbutz for four months was a problem.

> In the past, there have been requests from a *chaver* to be on a *sh'nat chofesh* and to remain on the kibbutz. But, up until now, we have succeeded in stopping this. Now, if a member decides to leave, he can live wherever he wants. But a member on *sh'nat chofesh* cannot live here– we have been successful in stopping this. There are people who think that we should change our rule, but I always say that a change in policy should be based on a theoretical discussion and not on a concrete case. I wouldn't want to make a decision based on your concrete case. After all, some people like you, and so they would vote for it, but others don't so they would vote against. This isn't a good way to make a decision.

Yossi further noted (threatened?) that it would be in my best interest to reach an arrangement with him, for once he brought it to a discussion in the *hanhala hachevratit* "there's no way of knowing what will develop." We said our goodbyes, and I got back on my bicycle and rode back 'home.' As I walked in the door, I said out loud, to nobody, but perhaps to the entire kibbutz "another nail in the coffin."

Before my conversation with Yossi, I had begun considering the possibility that I might not wish to continue to be a *chavera* even if I were to return to the kibbutz to live full time. I had been thinking about becoming a resident and *eshet chaver* (wife of a member). I had come to realize that the kibbutz was no longer satisfying any of my basic needs; it no longer enriched my soul, it did not give me a feeling that I was living the ideological life that I wanted to, and it certainly added nothing to my financial security. I see our kibbutz as having become ideologically bankrupt while remaining a bureaucratic nightmare. For years I have not had the sense of brotherhood or of equality or of justice or of the kibbutz being a light unto the other segments of Israeli society–the reasons why I so wanted to become a kibbutz member in my youth, and as kibbutz life was conceived in its early and formative years[1]. Instead, I see hypocrisy and pettiness, a desperate clinging to the perception of the past and an inability to see that the world is not the same world that it was when the kibbutz was established in the mid 1940s by a small group of dedicated youth, mostly from Central Europe, who had escaped the Holocaust, immigrated to Palestine, and came to make the desert bloom.

Thinking about the potential loss of my home led me back to the issue of the disengagement from Gaza and to my political beliefs concerning the Occupation. As the rhetoric and actions of the *mitnachalim* (Jewish settlers in the Occupied Territories) became more and more violent concerning the *hitnatkut* (disengagement) from the Gaza Strip, the *mitnachalim* switched from their pseudo–Holocaust based campaign to a shrewder and more sinister campaign. Instead of advertising posters of Jews being persecuted by the Nazis, donning orange stars, and shouting "Nazis" to the soldiers who came to remove them from their homes (well, some did so, but, on the whole, the settlers tried present a "saner" front)–the *mitnachalim* began posting advertisements that tied into mainstream Israeli culture, and traditional Zionist values, while showing the pain of being uprooted.

So, for example, they used a photograph of a container of *Tnuva*[2] cottage cheese that was conspicuously missing the picture of the "cottage." The words on the bottom of the ad read: "This is the way it looks when they take away your house!" Below this slogan, which was used in all of their advertisements, there was a sentence that stated that the advertisement was paid for by "*sane* citizens against the disengagement." The cottage cheese cover, minus the cottage (that is, the house) invoked the association of the traditional Zionist socialist value of having a deep connection to the land.

Another advertisement used the cover of a popular children's book, *Habai'yit shel Yael* (Yael's home). In this photograph, Yael's 'house' was missing. This book is a part of mainstream Jewish Israeli culture; the author and artist of Yael's house (Miriam Ruth and Ora Ayal) have written and designed a number of very popular children's books and they can be found in nursery schools, kindergartens, and many homes. I used to read this book to the children that I cared for, when I was a *mitapelet.*

The third poster was, perhaps, the most heart–wrenching of them all. This advertisement showed the words and music to *Hatikva* (The Hope–Israel's national anthem). The second verse (in Hebrew, the word for "verse" is *bai'yit* [house]) was cut out. This gave the message that not only have *Tnuva's* cottage and Yael's house been destroyed, but the heart of our national home–the homeland for which we had yearned for two thousand years–was being cut out by a (Jewish) Israeli government and military that were dismantling Jewish settlements in Gaza. (For the words, music and history of the national anthem *Hatikva,* see http://www.science.co.il/Israel-Anthem.asp.)

Not to be outdone by the 'sane' citizens against the disengagement, the left co–opted the 'sane' citizens' advertising campaign, and come out with their own poster about losing one's home. In their campaign, the metaphors were laid to rest; instead of a picture of cottage cheese, sans cottage, or a drawing of a little girl without her make believe house, they produced a photograph of a *real* Palestinian toddler whose *actual* (not drawn) house had been demolished by the IDF. I doubt whether the book, *Yael's House,* was among the objects destroyed when the house was demolished. . . .

I knew that I was not a Jewish settler in the Occupied Territories, who was being forced out of her home in Gaza in order to disengage from this occupied land, nor was I a Palestinian refugee whose house had been destroyed because it was built 'illegally' or feared to be a safe haven for terrorists. My story was much simpler: I was a *chaverat kibbutz* who had been told that by coming back to the kibbutz, where I had lived for my entire adult life, for four months during my *sh'nat chofesh,* was somehow an unprincipled act. A fifteen minute conversation with the *mazkir* had left me potentially homeless.

I have no photograph of the way that I feel, since the *mazkir* informed me that my home is no longer mine. All I have is an empty space where my love for the kibbutz used to be strong.

Notes

1. See information on the history and present–day realities of kibbutz in the article by Fidler (2002), who is both a journalist and a kibbutz member: http://www. mfa.gov.il/MFA/MFAArchive/2000_2009/2002/11/Focus%20on%20Israel% 20Kibbutz; an article by Rosner (2000) from the Institute for the Study and Research of the Kibbutz at Haifa University–http:// rsearch.haifa. ac.il/ ~ kibbutz/ pdf/trends.PDF and an article on new trends in kibbutz life at http://www. communa.org.il/kibbutz.htm)
2. *Tnuva* is the largest producer of milk products in the country and is also a co-operative that was established in 1920 as part of the *Histadrut Haovdim* [The Workers Union–The General Federation of Labour]–see http://www. jewishhistory.org.il/1920.htm and http://www.tnuva.org.il/ for details.

Chapter 11 or My Zionism, post-Zionism and confounded sense of identity

I cannot remember exactly when I realized that I was no longer a Zionist, but I know that this revelation occurred sometime during 2001–2002, the year of my post–doctorate in St. Louis and during the second year of the ongoing *Intifada*.

After being accepted for the Lentz Fellowship in Conflict Resolution and Research at the University of Missouri in St. Louis (UMSL), I left my family for an extended period of time. This turned out to be the first, but not the last time. I went to St. Louis on August 8th 2001. I think that I left Israel as a Zionist. The day after I arrived, there was a major terror attack in a Sbarro pizzeria in the middle of downtown Jerusalem, near the pedestrian mall on Ben Yehuda Street. (http://news.bbc.co.uk/1/hi/world/middle_east/1483492.stm). This was a Jerusalem area that I knew well, from the year that I lived in that city as a student, and from subsequent visits to the capital over the years. I remember feeling that I had made a terrible mistake of leaving Israel for such a long time and that I wanted to immediately return to Israel; I couldn't stand being away from my country when it was undergoing such pain.

Of course, I didn't get on that plane, realizing that life in Israel was going to go on with or without me physically located within its borders, and that terror attacks, and other social–political events, were not dependent on whether or not I was there. I had no control over such events although I had, and still have, this childish and magical feeling that perhaps I can somehow control what happens when I am close by.

That year was full of traumatic world events. The terror attacks of 9/11 occurred a month into my stay and I was called on by UMSL and by various organizations and radio stations, to talk about what it is to live with constant threats and events of terrorism, given that I was an "expert" in Middle Eastern terrorism. I had never thought of myself as such an "expert," but after accepting this role (it became clear that I really had no choice; people were desperate to understand), I was glad to have the opportunity to talk about the complexities of the political situation in Israel and to provide people with a perspective that did not neatly divide the world into good guys (the Israelis)–bad guys (the Palestinians).

It turned out that it was much easier for me to give these talks to non–Jewish groups; whenever I was invited to a university setting, or to a church, my words were met with nodding heads, acceptance and sympathy. However, when I gave talks to more mixed audiences, many of the Jewish members of the audience were uncomfortable with my criticism of the Israeli government, if not openly antagonistic. One elderly Jewish man came up to me after one of my talks and screamed at me: "With friends like you, no one needs enemies" and then walked angrily away. Another time I was told by a member of the Jewish Federation that she and others had, in effect, boycotted my talks since they had heard that I said things that were anti–Israeli (of course, I did/do not see it that way at all–anti–governmental policy–yes; anti–Israeli? Never.). She further added that because the mainstream Jewish community knew that I was "anti–Israel," I had never been invited by a Jewish group to give a talk. The woman apologized to me, saying: "I know that you are a nice woman and I *wanted* to come to your talk, but I couldn't. I hope you understand." It was the first time in my life that I had been scorned by fellow Jews and been labeled as an Israel (and possibly Jewish) hater. When I thought about it later, I realized how much this hurt me.

It is interesting to note that my "groupies" (this was the term that I used for the people–most of whom were well over the age of retirement–who came to all of my lectures, and always came up to warmly shake my hand both before and after the talks) were, for the most part, Catholics, who were involved in social justice activities through their churches. My other "groupies" consisted of left–wing Jews who belonged to Women in Black (see their website for information: http://www.womeninblack.org) and other peace organizations. These women, and one man, had been blackballed by mainstream Jewish community in St. Louis and were considered to be "troublemakers." One of these women, Hedy Epstein, a radical peacenik, who had lost her entire family during the Holocaust, but had survived because her parents sent here on a *Kindertransport*, became a close friend of mine. I was honored that this group of 'troublemakers' decided to adopt me.

While in St. Louis, I was on many list serves of peace organizations and received daily updates on the terrible state of affairs in Israel and in Palestine. Every email brought with it a testimony of another death, another injury, another injustice. These emails kept me in a constant state of depression concerning the future of my country. That was the year that many Palestinian ambulances were not allowed to reach their destinations after Israeli forces asserted that they were being used to transport terrorists. While this did occur in some cases, most of the time the ambulances were just trying to carry out their job–to transport the sick and the pregnant to hospitals.

When I sent out some emails to my friends and acquaintances, often asking them to write to the Prime Minister or to government ministers to protest immoral acts, such as these, that had been undertaken by the IDF, I received a number of angry emails in return: "You have been taken in by Palestinian propaganda. You've been away too long; it's time you came home and saw things the way they really are." One of my friends wrote me a long email about how her daughter's boyfriend, whose job was to check cars at one of the road blocks, did everything he could to be nice. She told me how he was kind to the Palestinians who passed through the checkpoint; he often brought them water on the hot days, or gave them shelter when it was raining. She took offense when I noted in my response to her that I was sure that this young man was nice, but that there is no such thing as a "benevolent occupier"; that this is a contradiction in terms. I stopped sending her my emails since I did not wish to antagonize her further and because it was clear that they were falling on deaf ears.

Somewhere, sometime, during that year, I realized that I may no longer be a Zionist, or, at least, a Zionist as it was defined and understood by most (Jewish) people. I understood that I no longer believed that Israel should be the homeland that gave Jews more rights than others and that what I wished for was a country that would be *midinah shel kol ezra chey'ya* (a country for all of its citizens). I am not a religious person, but if I have a deep belief in something spiritual, it is in my belief in democracy and equal human and civil rights for all. I could no longer explain to myself why Jews had rights that the Arab citizens of the country did not have. I could no longer explain to myself how it could possibly be democratic to occupy another people for 34 years–the length of the Occupation at the time. This was not my definition of Zionism, which, for me, had always included the very important component of democracy.

I was brought up a Zionist. I can trace these roots back to when I was in the fourth grade when we began learning conversational Hebrew and learning about modern–day Israel at the Sholem Aleichem school that I attended in the afternoons, after public school. How I loved Hebrew and how I loved the photographs of those young handsome *chalutzim* (pioneers) in our books! They looked so different than our teachers–many of whom were Holocaust survivors–and who spoke with heavy Yiddish accents and seemed to me to be very old (they were probably in their 40s, but to a young child, they looked and sounded *very* old). I could relate to these *chalutzim* and I began thinking about what life must be like in Israel, on a kibbutz.

We were taught that Zionism was one of the most progressive ideologies in the world and that it embodied everything that was good–democracy, socialism, equality, a love of the land and the need for a Jewish State in the country that had been our home, before we had been expelled two thousand years prior and cruelly dispersed throughout the world. (For an internet journey in Zionism, that includes many of the major writings on Zionism, see the Jewish Virtual Library website: http://www.jewishvirtuallibrary.org/jsource/zion.html.) We were taught that Zionism embodied everything righteous. Anti–Zionists, which included only Arabs, as far as I knew, were the opposite of everything good; they were presented to us, and perceived by me, to be dangerous, murderous, frightening and vehemently anti–Semitic. They had only purpose–to destroy the Jews and "throw us into the sea."

This was my basic understanding of Middle Eastern politics that existed for many years, even after I made *aliya* to Israel. I held this view even though I was against occupation of the Arab lands and thought it immoral to settle there–and something which I never considered doing.

Today I am ashamed of my naiveté, but even more so of my bigotry. I have no good explanation for why I was unable to see that that my perception of the Arab–Israeli conflict was extremely over–simplistic and deeply flawed. I was a peacenik, and spoke out for peace, but I held on to the views that Israel was solely for the Jews and that the Arabs were an evil people who had nothing but murder on their minds. I was a bigoted peacenik.

Perhaps my revelation that I was no longer a Zionist began to enter into my consciousness on the day that I gave my university lecture for the Lentz fellowship. I had decided to talk about a joint Palestinian–Israeli research project in which I had been involved that looked at Palestinian and Israeli non–governmental organizations (NGOs) that had worked together on environmental issues of joint concern (e.g. water management, endangered species, etc.) . My Palestinian colleagues, Prof. Sami Adwan and Dr. Fida Obeidi were in charge of the Palestinian side and Prof. Dan Bar–On and I led the Israeli team. I presented the project, which had begun in April 2000, but was cut short once the *Intifada* began in the end of September of that year. I explained some of the difficulties of working on joint Palestinian–Israeli projects, but was happy to be able to present some results and analysis of the joint work that had been done.

At the end of my talk, a woman, who along with her partner, was to become one of my very close friends, and who introduced me to the world of St. Louis social justice activists, approached me and introduced herself–Prof. Gerda Rae, from the history department at UMSL. Gerda told me that she was Jewish and that she had religious relatives who lived over the Green Line in a settlement, that had a name she could never remember. And then she said: "Your talk was wonderful! You are the first pro–Palestinian Israeli that I have ever met!" I was not flattered by that remark. In fact, I found it offensive. I remember stuttering something like:

> I wouldn't call myself pro–Palestinian; I am definitely pro–Israel since my criticism of our current governmental and military policies and the ongoing occupation is that they are immoral and having very negative effects on Israel–turning us into an ugly and violent society. My feelings about the Palestinians' actions are actually quite negative. My concern is more for my country than for the Palestinians.

I was hurt by her remark, as it seemed to imply that I must be anti–Israel.

I could not get Gerda's statement out of my mind for many days. I kept trying to understand why I was unwilling to be identified as pro–Palestinian; why did the thought frighten and trouble me so? I do not think that I have yet to arrive at a complete answer, and I still do not identify myself as "pro–Palestinian," but perhaps I can offer a partial answer concerning my difficulty in accepting this attitude.

This understanding is connected to two points–one more academic and one more personal/emotional. I will begin with the academic point. Herbert Kelman, a social psychologist from Harvard who was a child survivor of the Holocaust, has been studying psychosocial implications of the Palestinian–Israeli conflict for over three decades. Kelman has identified the phenomenon of "negative identity interdependence" (Kelman, 1999). According to this conceptualization of identity, Jewish Israelis and Palestinians seem able to only define their own identities in relation to an "enemy." For the Jews, the enemy is, of course, the Palestinians–who are seen as wanting to destroy us–and for the Palestinians, the enemy is the Jewish Israelis who have the same evil plan in mind. As Kelman notes, both Israelis and Palestinians are almost incapable of defining who they are, without simultaneously imagining and defining this negatively stereotyped enemy. Our constructions of identity are intertwined, yet seen as being totally separate and different from one another.

Kelman's (1999) concept partially captures how I construct and define my Israeli identity. One major part of this identity (though certainly not the whole) is connected to our ongoing and bloody conflict with the Palestinians. In some way, I can only succeed in defining myself as "an Israeli" by conjuring up what I am not. And while I am definitely not other nationalities–such as German– another identity that has extremely negative associations for Jews–what I am *most* definitely not is a Palestinian–whose need for self–determination and a strong identity often seems to put my identity in peril. Therefore, if I were to be pro–Palestinian, this might reflect a death wish on my part, and also be a betrayal of my fellow Israelis.

However, there is more to it than this, and this connects to the personal/ emotional aspects of my Israeli identity. Part of my fear of being categorized as "pro–Palestinian" is that, in doing so, I will not be *truly* Israeli–one of my most basic fears, given that I was not born in Israel, but became an Israeli only *after* I had made *aliya* to the country. As a result, I have always felt that, to some degree, my "Israeliness" is conditional, not a given. On some level, I feel it is dependent on where I live and how I express myself. I am afraid that it will be taken from me, or disappear, if I do not adhere to a mainstream Israeliness–one that does not call into question my loyalty or belonging to this country. Given that I am often unwilling to follow this mainstream Israeliness, that I have lived outside of the country for long periods of time over the last few years, and that I hold political views that are not always "popular," my Israeliness is in constant jeopardy of disappearing. And since I no longer think of myself as an American, this leaves me homeless and, perhaps, even worse–identity–less.

I am no longer a Zionist. However, I am not sure if I am a post–Zionist, because I am not completely clear on what this means, if I see myself as part of a larger post–Zionist group, and if I wish to define myself as post–anything. I continue to believe that we Jews need a homeland, given the grave harm that has been done to our people over the centuries, and that this state needs to be in Israel–our historical home. However, I find it morally unacceptable that our needs can or should be achieved at the expense of another people. We will never be free, as long as we hold another people in captivity. We will never know justice, as long as we act in unjust ways toward others. I believe that the answer to the Middle East crisis is a psychological answer, not a territorial one or a religious one. If we (Jews) are to know peace, and to be the light unto nations that we have always claimed to be, then we must understand that those other nations are not entitled to anything less then what we demand for ourselves.

In order to end conflict, one must be able to envision peace (Boulding, 2000). Once one is capable of imagining this peace, and seeing it as a real alternative to the world of war and violence, anything is possible. In my vision of peace, Jews and Palestinians cohabitate the land, from the Mediterranean to the end of the West Bank. Our shared capital is Jerusalem. We have two flags–a Palestinian flag and an Israeli one. We also have two national anthems–songs that celebrate the culture and history of each people. We speak two languages, Hebrew and Arabic, and we freely celebrate our Jewish, Muslim and Christian holidays. We live in peace.

This is the identity that I would like to have. An identity built on peace, not on war. An identity built on inclusiveness and acceptance, of the acknowledged legitimacy of the rights of the Jews and Palestinians to live as free human beings in their home.

Inshalla–B'ezrat HaShem–God willing. . . ..

Chapter 12 or Another soccer *Shabbat*

Israel has always been a country at war. We are a militaristic society–one that honors, respects, indeed reveres soldiers, guns, weapons, helicopters, planes and tanks. Given that we have been at war with external enemies since November 1947, when the UN decided to partition Palestine into a Jewish state and an Arab state (Bickerton & Klausner, 2001), it should not be surprising that we have evolved into a society that suffers from internal violence, within the Green Line as well. There is violence between Jews and Arabs (citizens of Israel), *Ashkenazim* and *Mizrachim* ("Easterners"–*Sephardim), dati'im* and *chilonim* (religious and secular Jews), men and women, as in cases of rape and domestic violence, the political right and left, *Rusim* (the generic term for all immigrants from the CIS) and Ethiopians, among drivers in traffic, and between soccer teams, such as *B'nei Sachnin*–that comes from an Arab town in Israel–and *Hapoel Tel Aviv*–that comes from the largest city in the country.

The idea that militarism has very negative effects *within* a society that finds itself often at war with an external enemy is not a new one. It was put forth by Spencer 140 years ago, who, in the latter half of the nineteenth century, saw the growth of militarism within Europe as being the underlying cause of social regression. As Spencer (1884/1969) asserted, chronic war generates a militant type of structure, not only among soldiers, but also throughout the society as a whole. Israel has been no exception to this rule.

Here is a story about everyday internal Israeli violence: When I was on my post–doctorate in St. Louis (2001–2002), during the second year of the second *Intifada*, I came home for winter break. One day I went to BGU to meet with some friends. At the end of the day, I walked over to the bus stop to catch a bus back to the central bus station. The number 8 pulled up, and I got on. The fare at the time was 3.10 NIS, and that was the change that I thought I had given the driver. However, it turned out that I had made a mistake, and instead of giving him 10 *agurot* (one tenth of a shekel), I had given him three *shkalim* and a penny instead. The driver immediately began *yelling* at me–what did I think I was doing? The fare was 3.10; who did I think I was trying to get away with paying only three shekel? I looked at him, quite taken aback, and scared a bit by his anger; I told him that I had made a mistake and would give him the missing money, which I quickly did. Where did all that anger come from? What could make a bus driver *so* angry over a missing 10 *agurot*, which was equal to less than two and a half cents?

After I gave him the money, he continued to mutter under his breath, but I sat down quickly and tried to ignore him. Two blocks later, an old man, who looked to be in his eighties, rang the bell for his stop. Before the bus driver pulled into the stop, the old man got up from his seat to make his way to the door, probably based on his past experiences that Israeli bus drivers do not always wait as long as they should for people to disembark. The driver, who I could tell was already angry, made an abrupt stop, and the man slipped and fell. Immediately people on the bus started yelling at the bus driver: "Why do you stop so abruptly?! There's an old man here! Somebody could get hurt!" Then the bus driver began yelling back, at the old man and at the passengers: "Why did you get out of your seat before I stopped?! You need to stay seated until I stop! Don't tell me how to drive! Mind your own business!" Everyone was yelling at everyone, and nobody went to help the old man, who was trying desperately to get up from the floor.

I was happy when that 10 minute bus ride ended.

I had about half an hour until my bus was scheduled to leave for the kibbutz, so I went to a *kiosk* to buy a diet coke. A man came up from behind and asked for an ice cream cone, and put some money down, before I had the chance to pay for my order. While I was taking out my money, he began yelling at the cashier: "Where's my ice cream? How long does someone have to wait?! I gave you my money!" I didn't tell the man that I was in line, and that the cashier was helping me when he had pushed ahead. I decided that it was not worth getting yelled out, or worse, over my turn for a diet coke.

Violence is always there beneath the surface, ready to explode.

It is impossible to live in the type of environment in which we do without feeling constant stress and anxiety. Like the majority of Israelis, I have a constant low level of worry, even in times of relative 'peace': When and where is the next bus going to be blown up? Should I take a taxi to the university, or brave the bus? (For the last number of years, I have only taken taxis when inside cities.) How many soldiers at a checkpoint are going to be killed when a suicide bomber decides to blow himself up? Will Daniel, who sometimes guards at checkpoints, be safe? When and where will the next kassam rocket fall in Sderot? When I drive to Tel Aviv, should I take the faster road that passes by that town or should I take the slightly longer route via another junction, just to be safe?

The randomness of the attacks and the inability to design a full proof plan that will keep you out of harm's way makes for very nervous people. And when we are constantly surrounded by images of war–such as soldiers and guns–and inundated with half hour radio and television news reports throughout the day about this or that danger–it is impossible to get away from the tension and the war.

For many years, the violence was pretty much contained to the enemy; our hate was directed toward the Arabs. Our soldiers fought soldiers from the Arab armies, and later on, during the first *Intifada,* the Palestinians. Internal conflicts were kept to a minimum, or more exactly, left to brew latently, as Jewish Israelis fought an external common enemy.

Here and there, however, there were signs of violence between Jews. One clear sign that internal strife *was* brewing among the Jews was the appearance of the Israeli civil rights movement in the early 1970s that called itself *Hapanterim Hashchorim* (the Black Panthers)–who had adopted their name from the Black Panthers in the United States. *Hapanterim* were young *Mizrachim*, whose families had emigrated from Northern Africa, mostly from Morocco, and Asia in the end of the 1940s and early 1950s. These second generation Israelis, whose families and ethnic groups had experienced economic, educational, social and political discrimination by the *Ashkenazi* elite since their immigration, held vocal and violent demonstrations, demanding full enfranchisement into Israeli society (Kramer, 2002). During the first Black Panther demonstration, held outside the Jerusalem city council building, the leaders were arrested on orders from the then Prime Minister, Golda Meir. From his office window, Teddy Kollek, who was the mayor of Jerusalem, yelled at the demonstrators: "Get off the lawn!" *Hapanterim Hashchorim* quickly became a household name, and their numbers grew, forcing Golda Meir to meet with the "troublemakers." As a result of this meeting, Meir made her famous statement: "They aren't nice." (Kramer, 2002)

No, they were not very nice–just as the *Askhenazi* elite had not been very nice to them for over 20 years.

The appearance, but also, unfortunately, quick demise of *Hapanterim* helped transform the latent *Ashkenazi–Mizrachi* conflict into a manifest one, and occupied Israeli society in the 1990s with the emergence of *Shas*–a *Haredi Mizrachi* political party. *Shas* has often invoked cries of ongoing discrimination against *Mizrachim*, in general, and religious *Mizrachim*, in particular. *Shas'* popularity among mostly, though not only, the working class and poor *Mizrachi*, grew to such an extent during the 1990s that it won them 17 seats in the 1999 elections for the *Knesset* (Jewish Virtual Library, 2004). We secular *Ashkenazim* became very worried about the way Israel seemed to be moving.

On our kibbutz, we have also had a few short instances of extreme verbal violence and animosity between *Mizrachim* and *Ashkenazim*. Most of our members are *Ashkenazim;* their origins are from Bulgaria, Poland, Northern America, Argentina, the Ukraine, Germany, and France. In 1972, our kibbutz absorbed a *ga'arin* (a group of young people, from a youth movement, who came to the kibbutz to become *chaverim*) in which a number of their members were *Mizrachim* whose families had come from Morocco, Algiers and Iraq. This group included members from both the first generation, that is, they were born in Northern Africa/Asia, and from the second generation, that is, born in Israel to *Mizrachi* parents. At times, the members of this group, along with a few other members of *Mizrachi* descent, from Libya and Tunisia, that have joined over the years, have asserted that certain *Ashkenazi* members are racists and that the *mosdot* (the "institutions"–people in power) "*dofkim et haschorim*" ("are screwing the Blacks").

One such incident took place in the beginning of the 1990s when a member, who came from Iraq, demanded that he be present when one of the older *Ashkenazi* members, was in charge of counting the votes for a kibbutz election. Avi insisted that Eliahu "hates the Blacks" and couldn't be trusted to count the votes correctly. These incidences have been far and few between, but they still run as an undercurrent in our community.

Just as women have never held key positions on our kibbutz, *Mizrachim* have been largely left out of power positions as well. There has been only one *mazkir* from *Mizrachi* descent; none have been *gizbarim* (treasurers) or *merekzei meshek* (economic managers). A *Mizrachi* (the same one who was *mazkir*) was in charge of the *anaf hasadeh* (the field crops), one of the two main economic enterprises of the kibbutz), and another *Mizrachi* was the financial manager of this work branch. A woman, who comes originally from Northern Africa, ran human resources for a number of years. However, this *tafkid* (position) has no real teeth; members, for the most part, find their own employment and do not consult with her.

As an aside, while this member does have an office, it appears as if she prefers to run her business from the *midrachot* (sidewalks); she 'catches' people on the *midracha*, when they are on the way to pick up their mail or to get their laundry, or in the *chader ochel* (dining room) in order to talk to them. This puts them in full view of other *chaverim*–making discussion of their place of work a legitimate topic for public conversation.

I never took seriously the cries of racism from the *Mizrachim* in our kibbutz. I saw their complaints as being an expression of sour grapes and as looking for someone to blame when the *chaverim* who made these accusations did not get what they wanted. I am not so sure anymore that this is so. If I think about my relations with the members who are *Mizrachim,* I think that, for the most part, I have had a certain amount of recoiling from them; they have appeared to me to be a bit too loud, a bit too impolite and uncouth, a bit too undereducated. My one good *Mizrachi* friend, Benny, whose family comes from Iraq, is a PhD and married to an *Ashkenazi* woman.

To a certain extent, I have been guilty of being a snob and, perhaps even, racist when it comes to the *chaverim ha'Mizrachim.* Except for Benny, I never really tried to get to know any of them, and tended to clump them all together into one bloc, or in Waller's (2002) and Staub's (2003) terms, deindividuating them, not being able to see individuals for who they are, but only as a member of a group with no special identity of his or her own. Perhaps this is also the reason that they never sought me out either, during all of these years.

Another kind of animosity (loathing?) that has escalated over the years in Israel is that between *dati'im* and *chilonim*. This is one conflict that has not impacted the kibbutz since we are a kibbutz of *chilonim* and while some members are traditionally–oriented, they see their religious beliefs as a private issue. This conflict has two faces, one more internal and one more external. The internal conflict has to do with what the *chilonim* perceive as *kf'iaya datit* (religious coercion) and the *da'ti'im* see as *chilul HaShem* (blasphemy). The external conflict concerns the growing hatred between the religious right and the secular left which have deep ideological disagreements about the "God given right" of Jews to settle in the West Bank. This is even evident in the names used for the West Bank; the religious use the terms *Yehuda v'Shomron*–Judea and Samaria–which is also the "official" Israeli term. The first face of this hatred is more internal since this conflict has to do with the non–separation of religious institutions and the State. I refer to the second issue as external since it is also directly related to our relations with and treatment of the Palestinians and not solely with relations between Jewish Israelis, though this conflict, to some extent, tore apart Israeli society as we moved toward disengagement from Gaza.

The violence and hate between the religious right and the secular left came to a head when Yigal Amir, an Orthodox young man who was opposed to the Oslo agreements, assassinated Yitzchak Rabin after a peace rally, on the night of November 4th, 1995 (http://www.rabincenter.org.il/site/en/rabin. asp?pi=7). The relationships between nationalistic religious Jews and left wing secular Jews have yet to be put right.

I do not know if I will ever forgive the nationalistic religious Jews for what they have brought upon my country.

The assassination of Rabin, and the days that followed, were among the saddest days that I have spent in my life, and certainly among the saddest days of my life in Israel. On my bedroom wall, I have photographs of my family from different years. One picture is of my father and Yitzchak Rabin, which was taken when Rabin was the Ambassador to the United States and my father worked as a fund raiser for Israel in the UJA (the United Jewish Appeal). My father and Rabin are standing next to one another, looking at the cameraman, and I like to believe, looking at me.

During the week after the assassination, people of all ages and from all parts of the country descended upon the *kikar* (square–used to refer specifically to the *kikar* where Rabin was shot) to light candles in his memory, decorate the walls with graffiti of peace and mourning, and to sing Israeli folk songs and songs of peace together. One week after the assassination, many of us from the kibbutz went to the *kikar* for a memorial service. Imagine hundreds of thousands of people and being able to hear a pin drop. More songs, more tears.

It's hard to describe in words the depths of the grief of that period. I obsessively listened to two songs that came to symbolize the murder and the pain: The first one was *Shir Lashalom* (The Song for Peace)–the song that Rabin sang, along with other dignitaries on the stage, at the end of the peace demonstration–minutes before he was killed. The paper with the words to the song, which Rabin had folded and put into the breast jacket pocket, was covered with blood and was shown repeatedly on the news. The second song that I could not stop singing and listening to was *Livkot Lecha* (To cry for you) which was written by the pacifist, Aviv Gefen (1995). Although Gefen had written the song in memory of a friend who had died in an accident, it came to be completely associated with Rabin's death.

Israel has never been the same since the *retzach* (killing, assassination) and the hatred and violence between the right and left, the religious and the secular, continues to grow. If there is ever disengagement from the West Bank, there are worries if there will be a *milchemet ezrachim* (Civil War) between the Jews, and *how* bloody such a civil war would be.

When I first came to the country in 1970, I was often frightened by the expressions of violence that I saw around me. Over time, however, I found myself getting used to these expressions of violence that were not part of the Midwest culture in which I grew up. I learned how to deal with people forcibly pushing themselves onto the busses, and elbowing me out of their way. I got used to the extremely vocal political arguments on public busses between bus drivers and passengers about what kind of Prime Minister Ben Gurion had been. I've become accustomed to hearing about how soccer fans acted violently after their games on Saturday. What I never envisioned was that Jews would kill Jews.

Chapter 13 or *Shira b'tzibur* – All together now

Not only is Israel a society of war, but it is also a society of song. After looking for something to watch on television one Saturday night a number of years ago, when it seemed to me that all of the stations (well, there were really only three stations back then; it was in the days before cable television) were showing local programs that had one group of singers or another, I joked that Israel must have 1000 singers per 1000 meters. One mythological description of the Israeli army states: *Anachnu yorim u'bochim*–we shoot and cry. I think this can also be amended to: A*nachnu yorim v'sharim*–we shoot and sing. . . .

When Yitzchak Rabin was assassinated, the country responded with song. Hundreds of thousands people gathered in the *kikar* (square), pouring over into the surrounding neighborhood streets for the memorial service. We came to mourn and grieve; we came to sing. This became the traditional way of commemorating Rabin's assassination.

One of Israel's most popular cultural activities is *shira b'tzibur* (community or public singing) (Almog, 2000). Every kibbutz, moshav and town that takes itself seriously has *shira b'tzibur* on at least one of its yearly holidays. The singers–usually no more than two–who come to lead the event not only come with a keyboard or tape with playback, but also with hundreds of slides with words to popular and traditional Israeli songs. In the olden days, the accordion was the instrument of choice; at times, a singer will still come with an accordion, but this has become quite rare. One song leads into the next, without break. The *shira* (singing) can take place on a small stage with people sitting on chairs, and can be held inside or outside–depending on weather and location–or with people sitting around small tables, enjoying refreshments and drink as they sing. At times, people are invited up to the stage to lead a song, or a microphone is passed around the audience for volunteers. It is not considered good form to "hog" the microphone; *shira b'tzibur* is a very egalitarian event.

Given that there are thousands of Hebrew songs to choose from, the choice of songs for the particular evening is decided upon depending on the specifics of the event. The singers can focus on traditional Israeli folk songs, songs from the different Army musical groups, pseudo-*Mizrachi* music; *musika salonit* ("salon music"–usually referring to dance music from the 1950s, 60s, and 70s), songs connected to the seasons/holidays, etc. While some of the more daring people might get up and dance a bit to the music, most people stay put in their chairs, swaying back and forth.

The Israeli icon of *shira b'tzibur* is Saraleh Sharon–originally a kibbutznik from one of the oldest kibbutzim in the north. I have never understood why people like her; her piano playing is very simple and monotonous, her voice is quite ordinary, and I find her incessant smile to be more than annoying. When the daughter of close friends got married a few years ago, in one of the oldest and most traditional of kibbutzim in the country, Saraleh Sharon was at the wedding, since she was a close friend of the couple and we had . . . *shira b'tzibur*.

About three years ago, I participated in an evening of *shira b'tzibur* that I can best describe as an extremely strange, and yet somehow not strange at all evening, for a number of reasons. Before describing the event, however, a little background information is needed.

On our kibbutz, we have a *chaver* who is a *madrich ti'yulim* (guide/hike leader). Ron studied geography, education and Hebrew literature. He has been a *madrich* for 40 years–he began as an amateur but later became a professional. Ron is considered to be one of the best *madrichei ti'yulim* in the country and people, best described as his groupies, will often decide to sign up for a *ti'yul* if they know that he will be the *madrich,* regardless of destination. I love going on *ti'yulim* with him; his historical and geographical knowledge, and his ability to tie the location to literature, music, art and architecture seem to be endless.

There appears to be no crevice in the country that Ron has not visited and he always brings along his small bag in which he carries poems, which either he reads, or gives to one of the participants to read in the relevant spot, and his *chalil* (recorder) that he plays at least once during the *tiyul*. Ron leads *ti'yulim* for *vatikim* (senior citizens; kibbutz founders; "old timers"), children of all ages, organizations, groups and, of course, for *chaverim* of the kibbutz. *Va'adat tarbut* (the cultural committee–the committee in charge of organizing holidays and cultural events on the kibbutz) organizes a number of *ti'yulim* each year, and Ron is always the *madrich.*

A few summers ago, Ron led a Friday night *ti'yul* to the area leading up to Jerusalem. The theme of the night *ti'yul* was the 1948 battles, led by the *Harel* brigade of the *Palmach* (see chapter 9). Ron took us to different points along the way where the brigade stopped and fought, and told us battle stories at the foot of memorials to the battles. Walking in the quiet countryside lit with moonlight, with David and *chevri kibbutz* (kibbutz members), retracing the footsteps of these historical military figures that often assume mythological proportions in Israeli military history, was a rather strange experience. After we had walked a bit, and Ron explained what had taken place at each site, we got back onto the bus and drove for a short while to the entrance to a park. When we descended, and walked for a few meters, we came upon white tables and chairs that had been set up with tablecloths, candles, wine, cheese, crackers and vegetables. *Va'adat tarbut* had not only arranged this walk in the footsteps of *Palmach-nikim,* but *shira b'tzibur* as well. Our singer–leader had an accordion.

We sang songs that were popular during the days of the *Palmach* and the War of Independence, in the moonlight. The microphone got passed around, and some of the old timers sang out in loud and clear voices. The evening was very surrealistic; it was as if we were being transported back to 1948, although I don't think the *Palmachnikim* had late night dinners of wine, cheese and crackers on covered tables and chairs. Yet, here we were in 2003–three years into the second *Intifada* and many years into knowing that the *Palmachnikim* did not always shoot and cry–though, according to memories of soldiers from that time, they do appear to have shot and sang.

I love singing, and I know many of the tunes to the old songs–though I need the slides with the words in order to be able to sing along properly. I often know the first verse, but certainly not all the ones that come after. In my younger days, I tried to drag David along to these evenings on the kibbutz, but never really succeeded. He likes American folk songs, but has never learned to enjoy Israeli music the way that I have.

However, like many things in Israel, I have grown tired of this tradition. *Shira b'tzibur* strikes me as an anachronism. Not that I think that community singing is inherently a bad thing, or that it has no place in present–day community life; quite the contrary, it could be quite beautiful. What bothers me is that our *shira b'tzibur* is often a hegemonic anachronism that continues to ignore taking a critical perspective on the social–political contexts of the "good old days." It continues to perpetuate traditional Israeli exclusionary myths of heroism, *sabraness*, *chalutziut* (pioneerism), without incorporating traditions and music from marginalized/peripheral groups that do not fit into these mythical categories.

It ignores the bad of the new days as well in that *shira b'tzibur* is no less popular, and perhaps even more so, among the *mitnachalim* (the Jewish settlers in the Occupied Territories) than within the *kav hayarok* (the Green Line). The *mitnachalim* see their settlements as being the new form of *chalutziut* and Zionism. They place themselves alongside the heroes of the past. Therefore, it comes as no surprise that they sit on their very green lawns in their middle class settlements and sing traditional Hebrew–Israeli songs of heroism on the battlefield, *chalutziut,* and the good old days, while their Palestinian neighbors suffer from lack of water, lack of land, lack of basic needs, lack of civil rights, and lack of capital.

Shira b'tzibur is only for Jews, not for Arabs. A few years ago, a good friend of mine told me about the way in which she and her closest friends celebrate *Yom Ha'atzma'ut* (Independence Day). They gather in the night in a park, bring instruments and have *shira b'tzibur* all night long. They have been celebrating this holiday this way for over 30 years, since after they finished their army service, married and had families. Once, Rachel had considered inviting an Arab friend of hers for the evening. But before inviting him, she decided to ask members of the group what they thought. "They thought it wasn't a good idea; he might feel uncomfortable, might not know the songs. He would be the only

Arab; they didn't think it was a good idea." *Shira b'tzibur* is only for Jews, no Arabs allowed.

There is something magical and communal about singing together with friends and family. When you sing these songs, you can be transported back into time–to fields of wheat, to young *chalutzim* (pioneers)–when *avoda Ivrit* (Hebrew labor) was the Zionist ideal. What could be nicer?

Chapter 14 or Belonging to kibbutz in life and death

Since its inception, kibbutz has always been seen, both by its *chaverim* and by the Israeli public, as an egalitarian and socialist community, one which encourages interaction with the outside–non–kibbutz world and one in which absorption of new members is one of its main goals. Unlike some other communes in the world, such as the Hutterites, followers of Anabaptism who live in rural communal settlements in North America and who tend to isolate themselves from outside influences (http://www.hutterites.org), kibbutzim have always wanted to belong, and have belonged, to larger Israeli society, and have been an integral part of the society, culture and country. Not only have they continually held recruitment of new members to be one of their manifest goals, but, in the past, they also saw their mission as influencing societal institutions in order to fashion Israel into a society with a socialist tone, if not identity.

While kibbutzim would still like to increase their numbers by drawing in potential *chaverim* from the outside, due to the disintegration of socialist regimes and economies around the world, and Israel's economic and social policies of the 1980s, the second goal is no longer on the kibbutz political, social and economic agendas. Today many kibbutzim have remained so only in name, while adopting a capitalistic, individualistic and highly privatized style of life (see, for example, Avrahami, n.d.; Simons & Ingram, 2002).

One central Israeli institution in which kibbutzim have had a continued strong influence is the IDF. A number of high ranking officers, including former chiefs of the general staff–such as Ehud Barak, who was Chief of Staff, before he was Prime Minister, and Moshe Ya'alon, who was last chief of staff–have come from kibbutz. This is no small feat, given that the IDF continues to be a very integral part of Israeli social and cultural life, and in spite of its fall from grandeur, that first began with the Yom Kippur War and that has since continued, as evidenced by an ongoing decrease in conscription rates (http://www.carmelinstitute.org.il/YouthService/nysinisrael.htm). Kibbutz members and their sons and daughters, therefore, see themselves as not only belonging to their small collective, but to the wider collective as well.

After Daniel had been in the army for about two months, when he was still in basic training, I asked him if he thought that his kibbutz education and upbringing made it easier for him to adjust to army life than, perhaps, for those children who had grown up in the city. Daniel quite emphatically said yes, expressing that his years in the *tichon* (the teen community), in which the adolescents spend much of their time working on group projects for the good of the *chevra* (*chevra* = society; *chevre* = group/ "the guys"), made it relatively easy for him to do what was needed for his unit and to acclimate to army life. Since Daniel was accustomed to living with others, eating with others in a communal dining room, and sharing things with them, he did not see the need to accommodate others' points of views and behaviors as an abnormal or difficult task. Perhaps Daniel, in his own small, unconscious way, was influencing his fellow soldiers to be more communal in nature.

But this chapter is not about the effect that kibbutz life has had on the Israeli Defense Forces or on greater Israeli society; rather, it explores the issue of belonging in a kibbutz, mostly in life, but also somewhat in death. The reason for including the above discussion is that it highlights the contradiction I have often found within kibbutz society. While kibbutzim have gone to great lengths to stress the centrality and desirability of engaging in a socialistic and egalitarian way of life, for both those inside and out, to a large extent, it has remained an exclusionary society, one that permits belonging in life, and later on, in death, to a select few on a limited and conditional basis.

A personal story may help to begin illuminating this point.

After I married and became a candidate for kibbutz membership in the winter of 1974, and after I had worked with a *vatika* for a few months in a *beit yeladim* (children's house) in order to get some experience working with children, I was asked where I wanted to work permanently. My options were two: the blue children's house or the yellow children's house, both which had toddlers. While I can't remember which one was which, one *beit yeladim* had two year olds and one had one and a half year olds. I chose the one with the younger children, since I thought that that would be easier for me, given my still stilted Hebrew at the time and because from the little that I knew of the women who worked in these two houses, I thought that I would get along better with the staff of the first one than that of the second.

When I went to *va'adat avoda* (the work committee that at the time decided where *chaverim* would work), I told them of my decision; let's say that I chose the yellow *beit yeladim*. I was told: "Sorry, but we have decided that you will work in the blue *beit yeladim*. Rivka (another newlywed woman, who had grown up on another kibbutz in the north of the country–and was married to a *ben meshek* (a child of our kibbutz) wants to work in the yellow *beit yeladim* and her *klita* (absorption) is important." That is my *klita* appeared to be less important to the decision makers on the kibbutz than Rivka's, though such a direct statement was never made. After all, I had come from Detroit, in the United States, and there must have been little doubt that of the two of us, Rivka and myself, I knew more about kibbutz living than she did. . . .

I went to work in the blue children's house and Rivka went to work in the yellow one. I do not remember exactly how long Rivka lasted in that job, but I do remember that she was not there for more than a few months before she transferred to work in a different job, not one in childcare. Her *klita* seemed to have hit some snags, while I felt that mine was mostly ignored. Rivka belonged since she came from a kibbutz and was married to a *ben meshek* from our kibbutz. There was no higher status. I, on the other hand, did not and could not belong to the extent that she did, since neither my parents nor David's had the good sense to immigrate and move to kibbutz. We both needed to prove ourselves before we would be seen as *really* belonging, though I somehow felt that we would never be allowed to enter the inner chamber reserved for *bnei meshek*.

In order to understand the context in which this experience took place, it is important to look at the meaning of *klita* in those days, over 30 years after the establishment of our kibbutz, and especially, *klitat banim* (absorption of children who had been born and grew up on the kibbutz).

When I came to the kibbutz in the early 1970s, there were many *tz'iirim* (young adults); there were *bnei meshek*, young Israelis, and *olim* (immigrants) from North American Habonim. David was one of those *olim* at the time. Overall, the population of the kibbutz was young; the oldest members were in their mid to late 40s, and the great majority of these older *chaverim* had children who ranged in age from their teens to their young twenties, while those in their 30s had nursery and elementary aged children. Those of us who had come from North America were also in our young to mid twenties; about half of us were married and it was assumed that those who were still single wouldn't be for long.

David made *aliya* by himself, in 1970, when he was nearly 23, while most of his *chevre,* who were close to him in age, had come the year before in a *garin* to the kibbutz. For some reason, David was never given a *mishpacha me'ametzet* (adoptive family–all newcomers to the kibbutz were given such a family when they arrived, to help with their *klita),* perhaps because it was mistakenly thought that he had been on Habonim workshop before (his friends had, he hadn't) and, therefore, already had a family. Instead of formally asking for a family, David decided to adopt his own. He began spending Friday evenings with a family that had four children and that seemed to 'naturally' gather together a number of young adults from Habonim, perhaps due, in no small part, to the fact that, at the time, they had two beautiful teenage daughters. The father of this family was an educator and had been the *madrich* (counselor) of the Habonim workshop a number of times. They became my kibbutz family as well after I moved to the kibbutz. Most of our visiting took place on *erev Shabbat* (Friday night), before we went together to the dining room for our *Shabbat* meal.

While the kibbutz spoke of *klita*, and its importance, very little was actually formally done to further this important goal. Most of the *klita* came from Israeli *ga'rinim* from the youth movement–who began visiting the kibbutz during their junior and senior years in high school. When in the army, the group would spend a few months on the kibbutz, working in the *anafim* and spending time with their adoptive families. This group lived together in one of the areas set aside for such young adults, which was called the *Nachal*–after the name of the army branch in which they served. These *tzrifim* (shacks/huts) were conveniently lo-

cated near the swimming pool. Since, over the years, most of the *klita* had come
from either Israeli or North American *ga'rinim*, the kibbutz members believed
that there would always be a steady stream of newcomers to the kibbutz. And
since at that time there was very little *aziva* ("leaving"–referring to people who
had been members and decided to leave the kibbutz), the population grew stead-
ily and there were always many young adults around to breathe life into the
community.

On the rare occasion that a new *me'umad* from North America, who was
unconnected to a *ga'rin*, came to live on the kibbutz, s/he was given a *tzrif* to
share with a roommate–always an *oleh* and not a *ben meshek*. The room was
furnished with a small twin–sized bed, a tiny refrigerator, small stool, wooden
chair, an electric kettle, a fan for the long summer months and a kerosene heater
for the winter season. The male newcomers were also given two sets of blue
work clothes (the color of these clothes was aptly given the name "worker's
blue") and work shoes, while the women had to provide their own work clothes,
though we were given work shoes if we wanted them.

These rooms did not have kitchens, nor did they need them, since we took
all of our meals in the *chadar ochel* (communal dining room). Most of these
rooms did not have indoor bathrooms or showers either, though these *would*
have been very useful. . . .

So, belonging was easy. You came to the kibbutz; you were given a family,
a place of work, a place to live, a *taktziv* (budget–on kibbutz, basically spending
money), work clothes and shoes, a place to eat and a built–in and ready–made
social life. While the *olim* from North America tended to spend most of their
time together, and the *bnei meshek* and the younger Israelis from the *ga'rinim*
also tended to spend most of their time in their respective groups, there was
mingling and crossover, due to work and due to the fact that many of us were
very close in age. Some of the North Americans, mostly women, married Israelis, and some of the *bnei meshek* were girlfriends and boyfriends with the
young Americans, though very few marriages came out of these relationships.
After six months to a year of being a *me'umad*, you were voted on by the *asepha*
(the general meeting, comprised of all kibbutz members) for *chaverut* (membership), thus making belonging to the kibbutz an official act. It was an extremely
rare case that a newcomer was denied such a privilege.

To belong to the kibbutz–that is, to be a *chaver*–meant that you held certain
rights and privileges. Every *chaver* had to work where he or she was placed by
va'adat avoda and the *sidran avoda* (work organizer–whose job it was to make
daily work plans). The members worked six days a week, Sunday through Friday, six o'clock to four o'clock for men; six o'clock to three o'clock for single
women/non–mothers; and six o'clock to two o'clock for mothers. We also did
toranut (service by rotation) that was usually divided along gender lines–while
both men and women worked in the dining room during the day and at dinner
time, worked on *Shabbat,* and sat on *va'adot* (committees), in addition, the
women had *toranut* for cleaning the public bathrooms and the men had guard
duty, and the particularly dreaded job of *tfisat ofot* (catching chickens, in order

to send them off to market). Rights included a rent–free 'house'–which was often no more than one room without indoor plumbing–a yearly *takziv,* a *takziv* for furniture and curtains, use of kibbutz cars, if you managed to get one, voting privileges, free food and medical services, free educational and clothing services for your children, certain 'free' subsidized commodities (such as cigarettes, toilet paper, hygienic products, a daily newspaper, stamps and envelopes, *asimonim* (phone tokens) for the public phone, etc.), free use of the swimming pool and sports' facilities, and the right to obtain an undergraduate university degree. *Chaverim* needed to wait in line for this privilege, with it often taking years for a member to get his/her chance to go out to study. If you belonged, the kibbutz paid your taxes, your electric and water bills and *chaverut* (membership) in the *Histadrut* and its *kupat cholim* (The Sick Fund–health insurance). Life was modest, but no one who belonged to the collective thought of themselves as poor. You received the same services and budgets regardless of how well or poorly the kibbutz did financially, which provided a great sense of security.

In those days, belonging meant doing what you were supposed to for the kibbutz and getting what you were supposed to get from the kibbutz. The formula appeared to be fairly simple, with all *chaverim* being treated equally when it came to these rights and privileges.

However, there was belonging, and there was *belonging.* While there was seeming equality between the *chaverim*–there were also subtle and not so subtle differences that could be discerned. There was the difference between the *chaverim* who came from North America and the *chaverim* who were Israeli born. It was clear that the Israeli born had a slightly higher status and were given extra privileges, and these privileges were always couched in egalitarian terms. But above both of these groups stood the *bnei meshek*–the children of the kibbutz or *The Children of the Dream* as referred to by Bruno Bettelheim (1969) in his famous book on *chinuch kibbutzi* (kibbutz education). The *bnei meshek* enjoyed a special status that could not be acquired, no matter how dedicated a *chaver* or *chavera* might be. The children of the kibbutz had always been revered as something special–always seen as something *more* than the rest of us.

In general, on paper, the rights and duties have remained, although changes have occurred, mostly in reaction to life on the outside. There are no more 'freebies'; every *chaver* now pays for whatever they wish to buy and the demands put on *chaverim* are pretty much limited to their need to work. While during the first 40 years of existence, there were never more than two to three problematic members, who were called *parazitim* (*parasites*) who never seemed able to complete an entire week's work, the vast majority of members worked very hard, often putting in overtime, of which there was no compensation, for the good of the *anaf.* Perhaps it is because we got older, perhaps it is because we got 'wiser' (*no one* was *ever* asked to leave, or even threatened with being forced to leave for not working), or perhaps people just got tired–somewhere in the 1990s it became clear that one could remain a *chaver* in good standing without working, or doing one's *toranut.* While such a *chaver* may be the talk of the *midrachot* (sidewalks), this has always been the extent of communal or economic sanctions. So, it turns out that once one becomes a *chaver*, if a person never leaves, one's belonging is virtually never in danger. You may be talked about on the *midrachot* and scolded every now and then by the *mazkir* or another kibbutz official, but your belonging will never be called into question.

When a *chaver* does decide to leave, or take a *shnat chofesh*, which is usually what the *chaver* asks for before announcing his or her decision to leave, things change. It follows that since belonging is perceived as a totality, so is leaving. Leaving–or *aziva*–has always been regarded as a kind of betrayal not only of the kibbutz community, but of what is perceived as righteous or moral. *Chaverim* who leave are often talked about in negative terms; their failings are emphasized and their intentions often called into question. They are leaving because they always intended to leave and have been exploiting the kibbutz for years; they're leaving because they didn't get what they wanted; they're leaving because even though we gave them everything they ever asked for and let them go out to study and out to work and gave them a car whenever they asked for one and provided their children with special extra–curricular activities and turned a blind eye when they did not show up for their *toranut* etc. etc. etc. they are ingrates and they do not know to appreciate all we have done for them and they will never be able to make it on the outside and they'll be sorry they left.

The *chaverim* who leave also have their own mantra; we're leaving because this place is old fashioned and doesn't know how to deal with life in the twentieth (twenty–first) century. We're leaving because everything is a battle. We're leaving because people here are *parazitim*. We're leaving because we're being strangled by kibbutz bureaucracy and committees. We're leaving because though we wanted to stay, things will never change and if we don't leave now, when we still have time to make a life for ourselves, we will be stuck here forever. . . .

There is defensiveness on both sides, and an inability to see the other side in less than stereotypical terms. Where there was once belonging, there is suspicion and animosity and distrust. Where there was once "us," it is now "us versus them." For this reason, there have been very few cases where people have left the kibbutz without hard feelings, expressions of remorse for the years 'wasted' on the kibbutz, and accusations flung back and forth between the *mosdot* (institutions) and the *ex– chaver*.

But, kibbutz social life is not so simplistic that betrayal remains a betrayal; given that so many of the *chaverim* are connected to one another by familial ties, or by *garin* ties, with long histories, such anger and resentment does not last for too long. And *ozvim* (people who have left) often continue to see themselves as still belonging to the kibbutz, even if they no longer physically live there.

One phenomenon which has developed over the last few years is the request of *ozvim* to be buried at the kibbutz. This request has come from people who lived on the kibbutz for a relatively short time, as well as from people who lived on the kibbutz for many years. The request, which is made to the *mazkir,* is usually put in terms of belonging; the *ex–chaverim* feel that the kibbutz is their "real" home, and even if they have lived for years outside of it, it is the home in which they wish to be buried. Not everyone is given permission to be buried at the kibbutz. The request is discussed by a sub–committee that decides how to respond, and if the response is a positive one, they decide what the financial arrangements are going to be. Belonging in death is mediated somewhat by social ties, but more importantly, by money.

The kibbutz has its own cemetery; one that is not under the auspices of the *chevra kadisha* (Burial Society–the organization that is in charge of religious burials in Israel), which conducts funerals according to *halacha* (Jewish Law). Our kibbutz handles its own burials, and while they are almost always carried out according to *halacha,* there are often instances where the *chaver* or his family do not want a religious burial. In most cases, there are additions to the religious ceremony; *chaverim,* relatives and friends read poetry that the person liked, write a special speech in honor of the person, or play music. There is a kibbutz member who is in charge of digging the graves and preparing the ground and another kibbutz member who has taken it upon herself to take care of the grounds, water the plants, and keep the area clean. It is a sacred area, and though it is directly across from a neighborhood in which there are a number of families with children, one does not find children or young people 'visiting' the cemetery in order to get a feel for the history of the kibbutz. It belongs to the kibbutz, yet does not; it borders the houses of the living, of the *chaverim,* yet also borders the fence of the kibbutz–the outside.

There are also burials of *bnei meshek* and *chaverim* who have died or been killed during their army service. When a person dies in the army, then they are given a military ceremony, and the headstone must be a military headstone, one that has a certain inscription. This headstone cannot deviate from the prescription; regardless of cause of death or requests of the family, the military has the final say. So, when a *ben or bat meshek* (feminine) or a *chaver* dies during military service, their belonging to the IDF supercedes their belonging to the kibbutz. A tug of war exists between the two; with the State's institution winning out over the kibbutz's desires.

Belonging on kibbutz is not always easy–neither in life nor in death. Life and death rituals are often prescribed; belonging is conditional, based on the luck, or 'bad fortune', of your place of birth, and full *klita* is not always certain. Some people remain on the kibbutz and are never fully *niklatim* (absorbed). Some people who leave, never really leave. Their belonging follows them beyond the gate and fence of the kibbutz and sometimes back again, upon their death.

Chapter 15 or Identity and belonging: Disengagement and right of return

I began this book as a *chaverat kibbutz*, but am finishing it as an *ex–chavera* or in kibbutz terms, as an *ozevet*. Last year, before I returned to NSU, I was informed by the *mazkir* that the *hanhala hachevratit's* response to my dilemma is the following: either return from my *shnat chofesh* in the next month or announce that I am leaving. I would not be able continue to teach at a university in the United States and be a *chavera*. I was told that the two do not go together–either you are in or you are out, with no in between. Kibbutz can be seen to be a "total institution," where all aspects of organized social life are governed by the institution's hegemonic authority (Goffman, 1961). The solution to my 'problem' or request–depending on how one frames it–that I continue to be a member, even though my work takes me away from Israel and the kibbutz for months at a time–is that there is no solution.

In August 2005, within one week, the combined efforts of the IDF and the Israeli Police Force managed to dismantle all of the 21 Jewish settlements in the Gaza Strip and two small, isolated settlements in the northern region of the West Bank. In spite of the opposition of the religious right, the decades of governmental policies that supported and encouraged settlement and in spite of the doomsayers, approximately 8500 Jewish settlers and a thousand or so "supporters"–mostly teenagers and young adults–were transported from Gaza to Israel, with almost no incidents of violence. Within one month, all of the settlements in Gaza were physically demolished. On the kibbutz, however, the problem of finding a way to let one woman, who is working outside of Israel's borders, to remain a *chavera* appeared to have no solution. It turns out that Herzl[1] was partially right in his statement–*Im tirtzu, eyn zot agada*–Where there's a will, there's a way. It turns out that some problems, such as the evacuation of Jewish settlements from Gaza, were not as complicated as originally thought. The vision can become a reality. Amending kibbutz policy, however, is another matter.

Perhaps I should be grateful to the *hanhala chevratit*. In a way, they helped resolve part of my identity crisis. Since they decided who I can or cannot officially be, and since the kibbutz establishment has decided that I must leave, I need no longer wrestle with the issue of my confounded identity. The kibbutz decision helped me to clarify which part of my identity is more central, at least for the time being. Given that I was not willing to give up my faculty position at that time, then my identity as a kibbutz member must have been less vital to my sense of self than my academic identity. Perhaps I should be grateful that I now have one less troubling issue to keep me awake at night.

However, identity does not easily disappear or appear because another deems it so. This is true in my case, where though I was told that I must resign my membership if I do not return to live physically on the kibbutz grounds, my life still continues here since my husband and youngest son are here. Just as I cannot wish away the identity of the Palestinians, who claim that this land is theirs no less than it is ours (if they see it as being ours at all), the *mazkir* and the *hanhala hachevratit* cannot wish away my feeling of belonging to the kibbutz. I can be told that I must decide to be in or out, but my identity, with all of its complexities and contradictions remains my personal property, even in this (pseudo)socialist community where things are shared. The Palestinians are here to stay and I am here to stay. The Palestinians will not disappear because this would be easier for the Israelis and I will not disappear because it would be easier for the kibbutz to say that I do not belong. We Israelis and those *chevrei kibbutz* will need to come to terms with this.

Palestinian refugees will tell you that while they may reside in a refugee camp, this is not their "home." Their *real* home is in pre–state Israel, in the villages of Palestine that were taken over and destroyed, and ceased to exist after the 1948 war. They long to return to their home; to carry on their families' work and traditions. This is as true of the refugees who were forced to leave or who fled during the battles of the 1948 war, as it is true of their children and grandchildren, born many years later, some of whom have never actually seen or walked on the land that their elders miss so.

The topic of home, and the meaning that it has for Palestinians and Jews was very evident in an encounter, organized by a jointly run Palestinian–Israeli research center, PRIME, that brought together two Palestinian refugee families and two Jewish Israeli families in the end of 2003. This emotionally charged encounter took place over a weekend in Talitha Kumi, in Beit Jala in the West Bank.

As part of my research on the Oral History Project from PRIME, an independent Palestinian–Israeli research center that undertakes collaborative research and educational projects–I worked with an Israeli team that interviewed Jewish Israelis and their descendants who had been refugees either from the Holocaust or Northern Africa/Asia and who settled in lands where Arab villages had once stood. Our Palestinian partners interviewed Palestinians who were refugees from the 1948 war, and still live in refugee camps in the Bethlehem area. In each family that participated in this study and attended the encounter, there were representatives from three generations–the first generation, who were the actual refugees–a son or daughter, who were the second generation, and a grandson or granddaughter, from the third generation.

One of the central topics that emerged from the meeting was the issue of "home." It was fascinating, yet sad, to hear how the Palestinians and the Israelis had such different conceptualizations and definitions of what home was. On the last day of the encounter, the 11 year old grandson of a Palestinian man who had become a refugee in 1948 from his village in Beit Jibrin, which is where Beit Guvrin stands today, introduced himself by saying his name and age, and by remarking that he is from Beit Jibrin, although he currently lives in the Aza refugee camp in Bethlehem. This young boy talked about his "home" with no less emotion, fervor and longing than his uncle or grandfather, although he had never seen this "home."

His story could have been countered with statements by the Israelis that he was, in fact, *not* from Beit Jibrin, since that particular Arab village no longer existed after the end of October, 1948 (See www.palestineremembered.com; www.jewishvirtuallibrary.org). Thankfully, no one made such a comment which would have led the discussion into a series of accusations and renunciations and blocked the mutual sharing that characterized the meeting. The Israeli participants told the Palestinians: "We understand your pain and loss, but those lands are no longer yours, they do not exist, you cannot return to them." However, the Israelis understood that the *feeling* of home and belonging was real to the Palestinians who sat across the table from them, not only to the grandfather who *had* lived there, but also to the boy, who had never stepped foot onto this land, and had seen it only through pictures. Regardless of where Muhammed had physically lived his entire life, his sense of identity and belonging was tied to mythical Beit Jibrin; he could smell and almost touch its orchards and fruits; he could vividly see its pastoral images.

It was clear from the discussion that the Israelis had a different perspective on "home." One of the first generation Jewish Israeli men had also been uprooted from his home; he had been a member of a kibbutz in *Gush Etzion* (the Etzion Bloc), situated between Jerusalem and Hebron, until the settlements were overrun and destroyed by the Arab league armies. Kibbutz members were killed and he, along with others, was taken as a prisoner–of–war to Jordan. Like the Palestinians who shared the weekend with him, Avraham also spoke of the home that he had lost, and his middle–aged son, now a father of three, talked about how after the Six Day War, when the area had once again came under Israeli control, his family would take yearly trips to *Gush Etzion* where they would hear the stories of what happened there, both before and after the war, and to see what had once been "home." However, that was then and this was now. "Home" for the Israelis in this group was their kibbutz where they had lived since the fall of *Gush Etzion* in the late 1940s. Their message was that one could not turn back the clock; life went on. Israelis and Palestinians needed to learn to live in peace, alongside one another, but the "homes" of the past were no more; and "new" homes must be accepted and embraced.

New homes must be accepted and embraced. This may be an impossible statement to hear from another; this is a difficult directive to swallow. For a feeling of home and belonging can never be imposed from the outside. One can learn to live with a new situation, to manage with a new 'home', but perhaps, that is the extent of belonging, and this belonging will always be superficial and unwanted, to some extent. We cannot expect that being *told* that one's home is no longer yours does, in fact, make this telling into a reality.

In mid August 2005, we evacuated the settlements from Gaza. The 8500 Jewish Israelis who built their homes in the Gaza strip, and who controlled one third of the land, leaving two thirds of the 360 square kilometers for the over million Arabs pushed into walled refugee camps and towns (Geography and Map of the Gaza Strip: http://geography.about.com/library/cia/blcgaza.htm), still believe that the Gaza strip is their home and is their land. The fact that they have been forcibly removed and their homes and communities razed, as if they had never existed, does not and cannot change this feeling. They tell the newscasters on television: "This is only temporary; we will return." They look into the cameras and tell the Israeli audiences: "(Prime Minister) Sharon made us leave, but God will lead us back." They, like their Palestinian cousins in 1948, seem determined to replay history. They left their dirty dishes on the dining room tables and pots cooking on the stove. They refer to themselves as "refugees" whose right to determine where is "home" cannot be mandated by one government or another.

The settlers, the Palestinians and I all have something in common. The Palestinians were disengaged from their villages during the War of 1948, the Jewish settlers were disengaged from Gaza during two weeks in August, and I have just begun my forced disengagement from the kibbutz. We have all been told that once what was home is no longer home. We no longer belong where we once belonged. Life goes on and the wheel cannot be turned back.

I do not believe that the settlers ever had the moral right to build settlements in the Gaza Strip, or in the West Bank; their religious/historical claims to the land, legitimate as they may be, do not justify their ongoing exploitation, repression, oppression and colonization of another people. I know that the Palestinians cannot return home, since those homes in those villages have not existed for over 50 years. The homes are beautiful memories, but only memories nonetheless. I know that by deciding to pursue my academic career, I voluntarily gave up on the kibbutz. It was my decision to leave Israel's borders to take a job in America, and by doing so, I knew that I was putting my kibbutz home in danger.

However, I also know that belonging and identity cannot be mandated from above, from the outside, by another. We–Israelis, Palestinians, kibbutz committees, and I–must learn to find a definition of home and belonging that does not exclude the other, and that does not oppressively impose a hegemonic definition of belonging and home on the other. For while one's sense of identity and belongingness may be complex, and even contradictory at times, our identities and homes are intertwined, and these knots will not be unraveled.

Notes

1. Theodor Herzl was the father of political Zionism. His book, *Der Judenstaat* (The Jewish State) was published in 1896 and it set forth the idea of how to establish a Jewish state in Palestine. In his novel, *Old New Land*, Herzl makes this statement which later became one of the best known slogans of the Jewish State.

Bibliography

About the Palmach (n.d.). Retrieved July 26, 2006 from http://www.palmach. org.il.

Almog, O. (2000). *The Sabra: The Creation of the New Jew*. Berkeley, CA: University of California Press.

Aronson, G. (2005). Settlers losing the battle for Gaza settlements. Foundation for Middle East Peace. Retrieved July 26, 2006 from http://www. fmep. org/reports/vol15/no1/01–settlers_ losing_battle.html

Avrahami, E. (n.d.) Members' views on changes in the kibbutz. Retrieved February 27, 2005 from http://www.kibbutz.org.il/eng/articles/ 010304_ eli.htm.

Bettelheim, B. (1969). *The Children of the Dream*. New York: MacMillian Publishers.

Beit Jibrin, District of Hebron. Retrieved August 25, 2005 from http:// www. palestineremebered.com

Bickerton, I.J. & Klausner, C.L. (2001). *A Concise History of the Arab–Israeli Conflict*. Fourth Edition. Upper Saddle River, NJ: Prentice Hall.

Boulding, E. (2000). *Cultures of Peace: The Hidden Side of History*. Syracuse, NY: Syracuse University Press.

Carmel Institute for Social Studies. Background on military service in Israel. Retrieved February 27, 2005 from http://www.carmelinstitute.org.il/ YouthService/nysinisrael.htm

Ellis, C. (2004). *The Ethnographic I: A Methodological Novel about Autoethnography*. Walnut Creek, CA: Alta Mira Press.

Herzl, T. (1902/1997) *Old New Land*. Princeton, NJ: M. Weiner Publisher.

Herzl, T. (1896/1946). *The Jewish State*. American Zionist Emergency Council. Retrieved August 25, 2006 from http://www.jewishvirtuallibrary.org/ jsource/Zionism/herzl2.html

Goffman, E. (1961). *Asylums: Essays on the Social Situation of Mental Patients and Other Inmates*. Garden City, NY: Anchor.

Ingram, P. & Simons, T. (2000). State Formation, Ideological Competition, and the Ecology of Israeli Workers' Cooperatives, 1920–1992. Administrative Science Quarterly. Retrieved February 27, 2005 from http:// www. findarticles.com/p/articles/mi_m4035/is_1_45/ai_ 3018120

Jewish Virtual Library. Operation Yoav. Retrieved August 25, 2005 from Jew-
       ish Virtual Library. http://www.jewishvirtualibrary.org/jsource/History
       /Yoav.html
Jewish Virtual Library. Shas. Retrieved January 30, 2005 from http://www. jew-
       ishvirtuallibrary.org/ jsource/ Politics/shas.html
Kelman, H. (1999). Transforming the relationship between former enemies: A
       social–psychological analysis. In R. Rothstein (Ed.), *After the Peace:
       Resistance & Reconciliation.* (pp.193–205). London: Lynne Rienner.
Kfar Etzion Remembered: A History of Gush Etzion and the Massacre of Kfar
       Etzion. Retrieved August 26, 2005 from http://www.zionism–israel.
       com /Gush_Etzion_Massacre.htm
Khalidi, W. (1992). *All That Remains: The Palestinian Villages Occupied and
       Depopulated by Israel in 1948.* Institute for Palestine Studies.
Kibbutzim site. Retrieved February 27, 2005 from http://www.kibbutz.org.il/
       eng/welcome.htm.
Kidron, P. (Ed.) (2004). *Refusenik! Israel's Soldiers of Conscience.* London: Zed
       Books.
Kislev, Y. (2000). Recent experience with agricultural cooperatives in Israel.
       Hebrew University. Retrieved February 27, 2005 from http:// depart-
       ments.agri.huji.ac.il/ economics/ cooperatives. pdf
Kramer, A. (2002). On the 30th anniversary of the Black Panthers movement in
       Israel. Retrieved January 30, 2005 from http://www.marxist.com/ Mid-
       dleEast/israeli_black_panthers.html
Lieblich, A. (2004). *Seder Nashim* (Women's Order). Tel Aviv: Shocken Press.
       [in Hebrew]
Milne, A.A. (1958). *The World of Christopher Robin.* New York, NY: E.P. Dut-
       ton & Co., Inc.
Mellul, C. (1984).The milk sector in Israel. The Institute for Advanced Political
       and Strategic Studies http://www.iasps.org/mellul.htm. Retrieved Au-
       gust 13, 2005
Moynahan, B. (1994). *The Russian Century: A History of Last Hundred Years.*
       New York, NY: Random House.
Pail, M. & Isseroff, A. (1998). Deir Yassin: Meir Pail's eyewitness account. Re-
       trieved July 26, 2006 from http://www.ariga.com/peacewatch/dy/dy-
       pail.htm
Rosenfeld, M. (2004). *Confronting the Occupation: Work, Education and Po-
       litical Activism of Palestinian Families in a Refugee Camp.* Stanford,
       CA: Stanford University Press.
Ruth, M. & Ayal, O. (n.d.) *Habayit shel Yael* (Yael's House). Tel Aviv: Sifriat
       Poalim. (in Hebrew)
Segev, T. (1993). *The Seventh Million: The Israelis and the Holocaust.* New
       York, NY: Hill and Wang.

Simons, T. & Ingram, P. (2002). Enemies of the state: Interdependence between institutional forms and the ecology of the kibbutz, 1910 – 1997. Stanford Graduate School of Business. Retrieved February 28, 2005 from http://www.gsb.stanford.edu/facseminars/conferences/oe_conf/pdfs/kib found.pdf

Spencer, H. (1884/1969). *The Man versus the State with Six Essays on Government, Society and Freedom.* Penguin Books.

Staub, E. (2003). *The Psychology of Good and Evil.* New York, NY: Cambridge University Press.

Taylor, J. (1971). *You've Got a Friend.* http://www.jamestaylor.com Retrieved July 26, 2006.

The Hutterian Brethren. Retrieved February 20, 2005 from http://www.hutterites.org/

The Liberation of Bergen Belsen. Retrieved august 14, 2005 from http:// www. scrapbookpages.com./ Bergen–Belsen/ BergenBelsen05.html

The Rabin Center. The assassination. Retrieved January 31,2005 from http:// www.rabincenter.org.il/site/en/homepage.asp

Waller, J. (2002). *Becoming Evil: How Ordinary People Commit Genocide and Mass Killing.* New York, NY: Oxford University Press.

Index

About the author

Julia Chaitin received her Ph.D. in Social Psychology (in the Department of Behavioral Sciences) from Ben Gurion University of the Negev in Beer Sheva, Israel. Her research has three main foci: (1) the long–term psychosocial impact of the Holocaust on survivors and their families and on young adults; (2) joint Palestinian–Israeli psychosocial research and (3) issues of ethnic belonging and identity among refugee/immigrant populations. Dr. Chaitin specializes in qualitative research, basing her work on narrative research, ethnography, storytelling and inter–group facilitation. She has published extensively in these fields. In 2001–2002, Chaitin held the Lentz Post Doctoral Fellowship in Peace and Conflict Resolution Research at the University of Missouri, St. Louis. From 2003–2006, she was Assistant Professor of Conflict Resolution and Peace Studies at Nova Southeastern University in Florida. Dr. Chaitin is currently a Senior Lecturer at the Sapir College in Israel. She continues to be active in peace and social justice work.